PETER ROBERTSON
PHEASANTS

Voyageur Press

For Noelle

_____

Printed in Hong Kong

97   98   99   00   01   5   4   3   2   1

Library of Congress Cataloging-in-Publication Data available

ISBN 0-89658-361-9

First published in the UK in 1996 by Swan Hill Press, an imprint of Airlife Publishing Ltd.

First published in the United States by Voyageur Press, Inc.
123 North Second Street, P.O. Box 338, Stillwater, MN 55082 U.S.A.
612-430-2210, fax 612-430-2211

Distributed in Canada by Raincoast Books, 8680 Cambie Street, Vancouver, B.C. V6P 6M9

Contents

Foreword

Fifteen years ago, on a winter's night, I drove west of Minneapolis-St. Paul, headed for Morris, Minnesota. Morris is a town of 6,000 or so residents located in the heart of what traditionally has been Minnesota's most productive pheasant country.

My intent in visiting Morris was to start a Pheasants Forever chapter. I was one of the founders of the organization that year, 1982, and in those early days Jeff Finden, another founder, and I would contact, usually through mutual friends, a pheasant hunter or two in a target community. When a connection was made, Jeff and I would arrange a visit to the town, arriving, it seemed, like evangelists, hoping our liaisons had spread the word and that waiting for us, perhaps in a school room or at city hall, would be ten, twenty, or thirty like-minded souls.

It always surprised me, as it did that night in Morris, when people who loved pheasants were willing to venture from their homes on the basis of scant information about a fledgling pheasant group. But show up they did. In small communities such as Morris, and even in big ones, say Minneapolis, jean-clad, boot-wearing straight-talkers willingly assembled on those nights. These were people not easily fooled on the subject of upland birds.

Our intent was not to fool anyone. Our message simply was that wildlife habitat, which has been in decline in America for the latter half of this century, must be redeveloped if we are again to have pheasants, ducks, and other birds in numbers we once did. Inherent in this was that federal farm policy must be more sensitively adopted and that farmers and other landowners must be educated about the value—not only to wildlife but to themselves—of leaving shelter-belts, wetlands, and windbreaks untouched. These are places where wildlife can flourish. They also are measures of the land's health—to the extent that they exist on the landscape or don't—which in turn is a barometer of humankind's ability to sustain itself.

Now, having read with great interest the following pages, I realized this Englishman, Peter Robertson, began his twelve-year study of pheasants at about the same time I visited Morris. "In that time," Robertson says, "I spent most of my working hours thinking about pheasants—how we could better understand them, and how we could improve their management."

Really, I thought upon reading those words. *Tell me more.*

Which in these pages, Robertson does. He writes about pheasants in America, for he has studied them on this side of the Atlantic. But most fascinating to me, as an American reading these pages, was the realization that pheasants obviously have engendered in people worldwide exactly what they had engendered in me, and which had prompted me—as if acting in the early 1980s in a kind of parallel universe to that of Robertson—to meet with people I did not know to discuss a bird we all knew quite well.

Robertson is a careful chronicler of the pheasant and pheasant information. He explains the bird's origins in China, which most Americans with an interest in pheasants are up on, at least in a cursory way. But Robertson also relates that the most common pheasant habitats across China are shrubs, forest edges, and farmlands. Marshland, Robertson explains, where many birds in the Dakotas and Minnesota live, are home to only about 16 percent of China's ring-necks.

The point, and benefit, of such revelations is that one can read this book as an American and come quickly to understand that the pheasant, a wholly transportable bird, is both fixture and chameleon. For example, in Britain, where Robertson conducted most of his studies, the pheasant is often considered a forest bird. Indeed, entire British estates have for more than a century been arranged so that driven shoots can be successfully conducted while pushing pheasants from woodlands over farmlands. This is no small feat, as any gamekeeper will tell you. Yet how different, really, is such an operation, in terms of what must be known about pheasants, from that of an uplander near, say, Pierre, South Dakota, setting out for a day of hunting on windswept grasslands, what an Englishman would call roughshooting?

Not really so different, Robertson tells us.

Nor is their much difference, continent to continent, in problems confronting pheasants. This nearly global bird needs nesting cover, flush with insects (and no pesticides, a problem in England as well as the U.S.) and thick enough to provide protection from predators. "There is hardly a crop that is not now sprayed with insecticides or herbicides, not to mention the fungicides and fertilisers that go with them," laments Robertson. "In Britain, at least, it was seen as a matter of national security to increase the quantity of home-grown food after the U-boat blockade of the early 1940s."

Whether a hunter of pheasants or an observer, the reader of this good book will find himself, or herself, transformed.

My bet is that, had Robertson gotten the call to be at that long-ago meeting in Morris, he would have been there. As it turns out, working in his "parallel universe," he contributed to the welfare of pheasants and the inspiration of pheasant lovers in an even more important way: By writing this book.

Dennis Anderson, Co-Founder, Pheasants Forever
Minneapolis, Minnesota
February, 1997

Preface

In the spring of 1995, I finished 12 years' work on pheasants, a fair proportion of my life devoted to the study of one species of bird. In that time I spent most of my working hours thinking about their lives – how we could better understand them and how we could improve their management. (In the first year or two I also used to dream about them, but happily that is something I grew out of.) One of the questions I have been asked most often is why anyone should spend so much time on one subject, surely there is not that much to know about a glorified chicken. I hope this book goes some way to answering that question.

I am a strange person to write a book about a bird that owes its present abundance so much to shooting. I have never shot a pheasant, or any other gamebird for that matter; and when I left school in London I had the typical urban dislike of hunting and hunters. Times change, and for the last 12 years my wages have been paid by the generosity of hunters or hunting associations. I have, however, always loved animals and wanted to try and understand them. As I have spent longer living in the countryside I have come to appreciate the role of game hunting in maintaining its character and the animals it contains.

I came to pheasants purely by chance. The final part of my degree at the University of Reading involved an interview with Prof. Gwylym Evans from University College Dublin. He offered me the chance to follow him back to Ireland to start a doctorate, 'on either pheasants or rats, we're not sure which we'll get the money for'. Thankfully, the money for rats did not come through.

Three years on a farm in Co. Kildare came as a pleasant surprise to a poor Londoner, and they settled me on research as the career I wanted to follow; I determined never to live in a city again. So, when I had finished my thesis I headed back to England to a job at the Game Conservancy Trust, still, I feel, the best practical bird research organisation in the country. There I started on half wages and a three-month contract until the result of my thesis was announced, and I have been there ever since.

At the beginning I worked with David Hill, who had been running the Game Conservancy Trust's own pheasant research and together we wrote a book on what we knew. Published in 1988, it now seems very dated and I know that, having just finished writing my thesis the bits I wrote bear the obvious style of a ponderous scientific tome: lots of statistics and graphs. I do not know if my writing style has improved but I have been determined to try and avoid the more obvious pitfalls of graphs, intrusive lists of references, statistics and the 'howevers' that are so easy to fall back on when writing about research. I hope that this book is more approachable. My apologies to many of my colleagues who may see their work reduced to unreferenced asides and oversimplified, but that is the way it is. Another problem with writing about science is that any statement ought to be backed up by hard data, preferably with statistics to prove the point. I am a great believer in the statistical approach and there is a time and a place for this. However, I do not think that this book is it, so I have entered into a fair degree of speculation as to what I think pheasants are doing – things I cannot prove. Nevertheless, I hope I make the difference between what is known and my own guesses clear.

Pheasants are also different things to different people. To hunters they are birds to respect for their quality as a quarry species; they are the livelihood of countless gamekeepers and managers; to birdwatchers they are often an unwelcome, alien intrusion into the countryside; to biologists they are fascinating in their own right. Whatever one's starting point, they are hard to ignore, and have had a real impact on the way farmland is managed throughout large areas of Europe and North America. When so much research can become just an end in itself it is a real pleasure to work on something that people care about and be able, sometimes, to make a difference. I am also lucky that so much of the pheasant's life has been studied by a long list of able scientists stretching back to the 1930s. The wealth of experience and insight that they have provided made my job a lot easier.

This book is inevitably based on my own experience and views, but I have tried to make it applicable to pheasants and their management the world over. I do not always agree with the perceived truths as seen from a particular region, but I feel strongly that pheasants are much the same in any country; it is only the people and the way they manage the land that differ. Instead of seeing pheasants in a British woodland as a different bird from those living wild in China or on the open plains of Kansas, I think it is far more interesting to try and understand why the same bird should behave differently in each area, to discover why it pays the pheasant to change its behaviour, rather than shrugging one's shoulders and saying the birds must be different. They are not different; they have just adapted and, in the process, given us a valuable insight into what is important for them.

Although I have written the text, the ideas, research and concepts in the book are rarely mine alone. During my years with pheasants I have benefited and learned from a huge number of people. Without David Hill, Ron MacDonald and Matt Ridley I would never have made it through my PhD. Ian McCall, although he probably does not realise it, gave me my first insight into what pheasants really need. Dick Potts, who views pheasants as a second-rate gamebird (his first love is partridges) has made me realise how important they really are and how I should prove, rather than just describe, what they need.

Nicholas Aebischer has helped me prove it. Maureen Woodburn has been with me through much of our time with pheasants and deserves the credit for much of the work. John Carroll, George Wilson, John Bissonette and Kevin Church opened up North America to me, while China would not be included if it were not for Zhang Zheng-wang. Count Alceo Bulgarini and his son, Count Maximilian Hardegg, together with Karl Pock and Allan Stokes, opened my eyes in their different ways to what wild pheasants can achieve. Doug Wise has been a welcome critic, Robert Kenward reminded me to enjoy research. At the Game Conservancy Trust I owe a great deal to many people for help, support and friendship: Nick Sotherton, Peter Hudson, Rufus Sage, Mike Swan, Kevin Wissett-Warner, Ian Lindsay, Andrew Hoodless, Clare Ludolf, Steve Tapper, Karen Blake, Roger Draycott and many, many others. John Carroll, Hugo Straker, Nick Sotherton, Jonathan Reynolds, Roger Draycott, Maureen Woodburn, Mike Swan, David Hill, Alexis De La Serre, Rufus Sage and Malcolm Brockless kindly let me reproduce their photographs.

Farmers and landowners have played a central role in our work, not just in terms of letting us interfere with their pheasants, but through advice and their role on some of our committees, keeping our work close to what is practical. Andrew Christie-Miller, Hugh Oliver-Bellasis, the Earl Peel, the Hon. Tim Palmer, Dick Riddle, John Hayward and Richard Baker have all given us their time and particular help. Roy Perks is particularly adept at bringing scientists down to earth.

Last, but by no means least, I could have done nothing without the support of hunters, hunting associations and sponsors. My thanks to the members and staff of the Game Conservancy Trust, the National Association of Regional Game Councils, the World Pheasant Association, the American Friends of The Game Conservancy Trust, Utah State University, Utah Department of Natural Resources, the Forestry Commission, the Country Landowners Association, Southern Counties Agricultural Traders, University College Dublin, Pheasants Forever, Tilhill Forestry, Jannsen Pharmaceutical, the W.G. Cadbury Trust, the Irish Forestry and Wildlife Service, the Department of the Environment, *Shooting Times* and *Cage and Aviary Birds*.

Introduction

I magine a bird that has followed man's development of farming for over 5,000 years, a bird that has shared in his expansion into new continents and been his companion in new habitats, and one that has been prized wherever it is found. Man's agriculture has cleared the woods, marshes, prairies and steppes that once covered much of the temperate regions of the northern hemisphere, and the birds normally found in these habitats have dwindled. Black grouse and capercaillie have retreated while great bustards have been lost from most of the European grasslands. In North America the prairie chicken and sharp-tailed grouse hold on but have withdrawn from most of their original range. Despite all this the pheasant has spread, carried by man from its home in China and the foothills of the Himalayas until it is now found throughout much of Europe and North America, apparently willing to thrive on the farmed landscapes that so many other species abhor.

You Pheasant...
You ornery, yaller-eyed heathen Chinee!
Who ever said you were a game bird?
Not the quail hunter, for you insult his dogs.
Not the pa'tridge hunter, for you scorn his
    forests.
The turkey hunter can't talk your heathen
    lingo
And the dove hunter says you fly like a
    plowhorse.
You're a brass-bound, hell-for-leather,
    unblushing roughneck,
And that's a fact!
You're shingled with galvanised feathers
And you spout cusswords when you fly.

You run a good bird dog all forenoon to
    work up an appetite
And likely eat the dog for lunch.
You'd spur the devil himself,
And when you're killed you're too mean to
    die.
You're even too mean for decent bird
    country.
You favor summers that raise feverblisters on
    rawhide
And winters that jell your cussedness at forty
    below.
You get fat on a ration of bobwire and
    blizzard.
Why, you're no game bird . . .
You're a cross between a cottonwood staub
And a Dakota dust-devil.
But out here in corn country
Where we've plowed under the prairie
    chickens
And planted eighty million acres to cash
    grain,
What other birds will put up with us?
You're about all we've got.
And we reckon that you're all we need!

What is it about this bird that has made it such a success? No one would accuse it of being particularly intelligent or an especially devoted parent to its chicks. It seems to fall prey to every hazard that nature throws at it, but it still manages to be a common bird of farmed landscapes wherever it occurs. Part of this success is undoubtedly down to man. It is man who has introduced it to new areas, hoping to provide game and a familiar sight in a foreign land. He is also responsible for nurturing it, creating habitats for its benefit, killing its enemies and, through his agriculture, providing the opportunity for it to thrive.

The pheasant itself is remarkable. While most birds are small the pheasant is rather large. While most have similar sexes, cock and hen pheasants could almost be separate species. Where most fly, the pheasant prefers to walk and lays its eggs on the ground. While it is dearly loved by hunters, many birdwatchers hold it in contempt. In Britain they once voted it the most hated bird and had it declared an honorary mammal to distance it from the others. It has also probably attracted more funds for its preservation, and for studying its life, than any other free-living bird (the domestic chicken probably comes first if one drops the 'free-living' condition). My own reference collection contains over 600 scientific papers written about this bird, and over 1,000 scientists have worked on it at some time in their lives, not to mention the multitude of hunting magazines devoting a large portion of their contents to different aspects of its life and management.

Man's influence is inseparable from the pheasant's fortunes. But it is too easy to see this bird just as a product of his interest, rather than as an individual species in its own right. I am a great believer in the idea that to manage an animal properly one must understand its life and needs. So a large part of this book is devoted to the pheasant's view of the world, what it wants and the factors that limit its numbers. For those who want instant recipes for managing pheasants I would recommend that they start elsewhere; this book is first and foremost about the bird.

The Americans call the pheasant the ring-neck, but many races have no white collar so the name does not make much sense outside North America. I will therefore refer to the subject of this book as the common pheasant. Its formal scientific name is *Phasianus colchicus*, a reference to the mythical visit of Jason and the Argonauts to the Phasis Valley in Colchis, part of modern Georgia on the Black Sea, in search of the Golden Fleece. On Jason's return to Greece he supposedly also brought back the first pheasants to Europe, possibly around 1300 BC. The Greeks, and later the Romans, appear to have kept them as table birds. The Romans certainly left recipes and accounts of how to keep them in captivity. They also left pictures, mosaics inlaid on tiled floors. There is a mystery surrounding many of these. The Georgian pheasants, at the extreme

west of their native range, are black-necks, with no trace of the white collar. Despite this, some of the Roman pictures show birds with large white neck-rings. Did the Romans also obtain pheasants from further east, the parts of China where ring-necked birds are common? The Great Silk Road, bringing trade from China to Europe, was certainly open in Roman times, and it may have carried pheasants as well. Another, more mundane, explanation could also have to do with the silks they imported. The Chinese love to embroider their fabrics with pictures of birds, including their own pheasants. Possibly the Roman mosaics were copied from imported Chinese silks. Wherever the birds came from, ring-necks or not, they certainly became established in Italy, France and parts of Germany before the fall of the Roman empire.

Whether or not they were established in Britain in Roman times is open to debate. There are Romano-British mosaic pavements from about the fourth century AD showing what are unmistakably pheasants, but these may be copies from Europe. Even if they had spread to this country they were certainly not common during the Dark Ages. More birds were almost certainly brought over by the Normans some time after their invasion in 1066. There are accounts of 'cocks of the wood' being served at banquets although these were very probably black grouse – it is impossible to tell. The next definite evidence is the Sherborne Missal, an illuminated manuscript showing a pheasant in the margin which was probably produced about 1400. After this, evidence starts to become more frequent. They were definitely breeding in the wild at the end of the 1400s, when their nests were protected by royal decree. Their range also began to spread, with records from Scotland and Ireland in the 1600s, and slightly later from Wales.

Although the spread of the pheasant through Europe has been a success story, it took the better part of 2,000 years to make its impact and records are fairly thin on the ground. In North America the situation could not be more different. In just over 100 years they have spread like wildfire across much of the continent, and their progress is fairly well documented. From a small start in the Willamette Valley in Oregon in the 1880s they are now found in over 35 states in the USA, nine Canadian provinces and a small part of Mexico.

Writing about the introduction of pheasants to the Western world is easy: there are fairly good records and a multitude of scientific papers describing what worked where. Just looking at the available literature, however, can grossly underestimate the importance of their native range. The trouble is that, although truly wild pheasants are found across much of Asia, there is relatively little written about them.

China has long been a great mystery to the West – a huge, ancient and secretive culture which has made itself inaccessible to much of the world since the Second World War. It is only recently that Westerners have again been able to visit in any numbers and to see the home of the pheasant. My own involvement with China started in the late 1980s when Zhang Zheng-wang, a young Chinese biologist from Beijing, came over to Britain for a year. Zheng-wang had just finished his masters degree on Cabot's tragopan, a superbly plumaged Chinese pheasant that lives in undisturbed forests. He was in Britain to visit some of our research centres as a guest of the World Pheasant Association (WPA). China is home to more pheasant species than any other country and WPA, an international organisation with responsibility for encouraging and supporting the conservation of these species, was keen to establish better links with their biologists. Zheng-wang came to the Game Conservancy Trust for six months to learn some of our techniques, and we were very keen to learn about conditions in China. In 1989, the WPA's attempts to establish links had paid off and it held its main pheasant conference in Beijing with Zheng-wang as one of the organisers. As part of the conference a field trip was arranged to a nature reserve: Pangquangquo in Shanxi Province, a forest reserve in a mountainous region. The reserve itself is famous for the populations of brown-eared pheasants which live in the forest, but around the edges are good populations of common pheasants. They live in the valley bottoms where local farmers have cleared the scrub to create small fields. It was here that I had my first chance to see native pheasants, sneaking out of our compound one morning to hear them calling from the hillsides and missing the official tour later that day to explore the valley. John Carroll, an American pheasant biologist, and I spent the day flushing birds from the small fields and clumps of sea buckthorn scrub that surrounded the farmland. The next day we talked some of our colleagues out of looking for brown-ears and drove the whole valley as if it were an English pheasant shoot, flushing 16 birds from about 60 acres of field and scrub, a very respectable density of wild birds for any part of the world.

Zheng-wang was with us for the tour and was considering which species to study next. With only a little persuasion from us he settled on the Chinese ring-neck. It is the most common of the Chinese pheasants and certainly not endangered, like so many others it is relatively easy to study, with a wealth of background information available from Europe and North America. His work would also be of enormous value to Westerners working on the same species. Those few days thus led to the start of a joint Anglo-Chinese study of this bird.

Prior to Zheng-wang starting work, there was virtually no information about Chinese ring-necks available in the West although, as we soon found, there was a considerable amount of Chinese literature that we knew nothing about. One of the first things he did was to send a questionnaire to other Chinese biologists asking for information about the birds in their areas.

There is a firm belief in the West that the pheasant is naturally a marshland bird. I have regularly heard hunters say that British birds living in woodland are unnatural and are only there because of man; left to their own devices they would only be found in the marshes as happens in China. There is no doubt that the birds do like living in reed beds and other wetland vegetation, but Zheng-wang's survey put paid to the idea that marshes are their only natural home. He received 84 replies to his questionnaire, describing the typical habitats used by pheasants across China. The most common answers (over 60 per cent of replies) were that they lived in shrub, forest edge and farmland. Marshland was well down on the list (16 per cent). It looks as though pheasants in China are using just the same sorts of habitats as they do in the West. They will use marshes when the chance arises, but are certainly not distinctively marshland birds or birds that will live nowhere else. This certainly backs up what we saw in Pangquangquo, where large numbers of the birds concentrated in shrub at the edge of farmland, with not a marsh in sight.

What we have then is a species that naturally spreads across much of China and Asia to the Black Sea. Thanks to man it is also now firmly rooted in much of Europe, North America and New Zealand. I have had the opportunity to see a variety of different parts of this extensive range, and to talk to others who are familiar with this bird in even more. Its flexibility is amazing. It is found amongst dwarf shrubs on Chinese mountain tops over 3,000m above sea level and in the wide-open prairies of the American Midwest. I have seen it on treeless, windswept islands on the exposed coasts of Ireland and off the north coast of Scotland, where the Northern Lights are often seen. It thrives in the fertile farmlands of lowland England and northern Austria, the Canterbury Plain in New Zealand and in the suburbs of Salt Lake City in Utah. What is it about this species that makes it so adaptable?

Despite the widely held view that pheasants in their native range are marshland birds, most Chinese pheasants are associated with shrubs, forest edges and farmland.

Austria

Shanxi

UK

Pennsylvania (John Carroll)

Utah

Kansas

Pheasant Habitats Around the World

WHAT IS A PHEASANT?

The pheasant is one of a large group of birds known as the galliformes or gamebirds; apart from the different sorts of pheasants, this group also includes partridge, quail, grouse, turkey, guinea fowl and a range of less well known groups. China and south-east Asia seem to be the home, not just of the common pheasant, but also of the many closely related but less well-known species: argus pheasants with their huge tails – the largest feathers of any bird; the bizarre tragopans whose chicks can fly as soon as they hatch; peacocks; junglefowl, the predecessors of the domestic chicken; ruffed pheasants, such as the golden and Lady Amherst; and many more.

In this company the common pheasant is a relatively drab bird; its claim to fame is its success in following man and its adaptability. Officially there are two species of pheasant: the common group and the Japanese green pheasant. These two species are then split into 30 and two subspecies or races respectively. These distinctions are based mainly on differences in the male plumage, and on the isolation of the greens on the Japanese archipelago. I have real doubts about the validity of this division into all these different subspecies. I think half the problem is that pheasants are such pretty and popular birds. Expeditions sent out to describe new species often liked to describe any bird with some slight difference in plumage from the norm as a new subspecies, particularly as they could then name it after their sponsor or team leader. So we have the Prince of Wales' pheasant, Rothschild's pheasant, Strauch's pheasant and so on. This is not to say that there are not distinct races, just that 32 is probably a bit excessive. I estimate that there are probably only five or six, although I could be wrong.

Brown eared-pheasants

The pheasant family includes a wide range of related but less well known species, such as the cheer pheasant, brown eared-pheasant, peacock and Cabot's tragopan.

Cheer pheasant

Peacock

Cabot's Tragopan

SUBSPECIES

There is a distinct trend in the male plumage of the different subspecies from west to east. Starting on the shores of the Black Sea are the colchicus group, also known as the black-necks, which were the first introduction to Europe. The males are typically purplish with light brown or buff wing feathers and no trace of a neck-ring.

To the south-east of the Caspian Sea are the principalis-chrysomelis group, the white-wings with their characteristic light wing coverts. The males are a bit redder than the black-necks and some have a partial neck-ring. Next east are the mongolicus birds from east of the Aral Sea, similar to the white-wings, but more coppery in colour and with a wide neck ring.

All of these groups have reddish rumps. The next race east, the Tarim pheasant, also known as the olive-rumped pheasant, however, is an intermediate race between them and the remaining eastern groups.

The largest group of all is the torquatus, the Chinese ring-necks, which include the remaining pheasants from the eastern half of Asia and are also known as grey-rumped pheasant.

Lastly are the Japanese greens. I doubt whether they deserve to be classified as a separate species, but it is hard to tell; they are certainly distinct from the other groups and even the hens are noticeably darker.

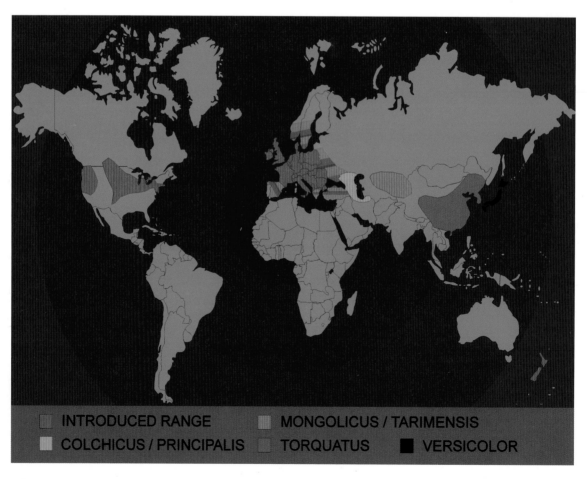

INTRODUCED RANGE   MONGOLICUS / TARIMENSIS
COLCHICUS / PRINCIPALIS   TORQUATUS   VERSICOLOR

Melanistic cock

White hen

Mutations, such as this melanistic or black male and white female are relatively common in some areas, particularly where birds are reared.

Another curiosity is the mule or gynandromorph, a female which develops partial male plumage following damage to the ovaries.

These different subspecies provide the basic stock from which the introduced populations of Europe, North America and New Zealand are derived. The spread of the pheasant has long been associated with birds reared and released by man, and during this process a number of mutations and oddities have emerged. The most common mutation is the black or melanistic pheasant. These handsome birds seem to occur throughout the range, including China, Europe and North America, although they are particularly common in Britain where they have been encouraged by gamekeepers. The males are very dark with their under-feather colouring a dark matt black. The visible parts of the feathers are a deep purple or blue-green and they hardly ever seem to have a neck-ring. The hens are particularly noticeable, usually being a uniform chocolate brown. They are very similar at first sight to red grouse, although quite a number also sport a white bib under the chin. There has long been speculation that these birds are crosses between common pheasants and the closely related Japanese green. Certainly, male Japanese greens have some of the characteristics of the male melanistic and it is easy to see where the confusion has come from, but this cannot be the answer. The hens and chicks of the Japanese green are really very similar to common pheasants. On the other hand melanistic chicks and hens are both chocolate brown. Crosses of common and Japanese green birds produce normal-looking hens and chicks whereas crosses of melanistics with either of these two groups produce half normal and half melanistic offspring. Melanistics are clearly a mutation.

Other plumage mutations include white birds, not true albinos as the males still have pigmented red wattles, and leucistic or 'Bohemian' birds with white under-feathers and pale colours and markings at the feather tips. I have also seen pictures of some spectacular captive Australian mutants where the cocks are covered in metallic blue feathers like those seen on a normal bird's head but covering much of their body. All of these mutations are only really seen on game farms or where such birds have been released, and I doubt whether many of them would last long in a truly wild situation.

Another curiosity that occurs with surprising frequency is the mule. These birds, although female, develop varying amounts of male plumage. In Britain they probably account for about one hen in 500. The best mules, or gynandromorphs as they are more properly known, can easily pass as males at a casual glance. They have the blue head, the bronzed body and, on occasion, the neck-ring of a male. A closer look, however, reveals that they have no proper wattles and no ear-tufts or spurs, and their tails are short and plain like a true female. They can so easily be confused that I once saw one in a Polish museum collection on display as a male. With the help of an interpreter and a bit of miming, I tried to convince the curator of his mistake, but I think he just concluded that I was a decadent Westerner.

Mules are not born that way; on two occasions now we have tagged hens one year and recovered them the next, to find that they had changed plumage. They also seemed unaware of their change and continued to act like females. A few years ago, I was counting breeding birds not far from my house and came across a territorial male with three females, two of whom had almost perfect male plumage. The cock treated them just like any other hens and they all seemed quite happy with their somewhat confused roles. In fact one of the mules returned to breed with the same male the next year.

I have had the chance to dissect a few of these strange birds which have turned up on shoot days. In each case they have been suffering from avian tuberculosis which has settled in their ovaries. There are also well-documented cases where the same effect has been caused by shotgun pellets lodged in the ovaries, although I have never examined one myself. There have also been experiments in America, which have shown that if the ovaries are damaged and stop producing the relevant hormones, this is what starts the change. In pheasants, this hormone deficiency leads to 'maleness' in terms of general plumage. The development of spurs, ear-tufts and the spectacular tail are under the control of another hormone, testosterone, which is why mules almost never develop these features.

Although it is impossible to be certain, I am fairly sure that mules are responsible for some of the reports of males incubating nests and being seen with chicks. However, they cannot account for them all. The Elvedon Estate in Norfolk has a clear photograph of a cock pheasant, complete with wattles, incubating a nest. He reportedly hatched them successfully, although he failed to rear the chicks. Some scientists working with captive pheasants in Pennsylvania during the 1950s, also found some males sitting on nests in their pens. Although there are no photographs to prove that they were not mules, it is unlikely that they would be confused in the pens. None of the males hatched any chicks and why there should be three reports of this peculiar behaviour from one study in Pennsylvania will always remain a mystery.

Females with spurs are also fairly common. These spurs are never as long as they are in males, and they seem to occur most frequently in old hens, although we have never looked at it properly.

Another oddity that I have never seen myself is the hen-coloured cock. In California there have been a number of reports of birds with the body shape and size of a male, ear-tufts, spurs, but no wattles and feathers like a hen. These seem to be genetic abnormalities; when dissected they were found to have a mixture of partially developed male and female organs. Such a striking bird would, I am sure, have been spotted in Britain if it had occurred, so it may be some mutation peculiar to the strain found in California.

Where then does this leave us? We have a bird that lives in a wide range of diverse habitats and in many different countries. Sometimes it is a native, more often it has been introduced by man. We have a range of different subspecies with considerable differences in weight and plumage. In many areas it is intensively managed by man, both as a wild bird and sometimes through the release of artificially reared individuals. Some people, often hunters, are willing to spend large amounts of money on its conservation, others view it as an alien weed that has no place in their country. Is it possible to make sense of all this variety and really understand the species in its own right? That is what I hope to achieve in this book.

Recent initiatives in Britain have raised the incentives for farmers to plant new small woods on their land.

THE WINTER

Late autumn and winter are the seasons during which most people know the pheasant best. For the hunter, it is the time when he searches for his quarry and learns most of their likes and dislikes – essential if he is to find the bird and to know what to expect on a shoot. Winter can also be a hard time for the birds and their choice of habitat can have a big influence on their chances of surviving through to the breeding season in the spring. What then do we know about pheasants during the winter? The habitats they use in different parts of the world vary widely and this in itself can tell us what may be important to them. A great deal has also been written about their needs at this time of year, with literature stretching back into the last century.

My first experience of pheasants' requirements started in the mid-1980s. In 1986, when I had just started working with David Hill at the Game Conservancy Trust, the main question in my mind was where my wages were going to come from for the next year. Fortunately, the Forestry Commission was changing its policy on new woodland planting, moving away from supporting large conifer plantations to a more environmentally sensitive policy of promoting small mixed woods on farmland. Part of this move involved encouraging farmers that woods were something they should be interested in. As many farmers enjoy pheasant shooting and small farm woodlands are an integral part of pheasant habitat during the winter, they agreed to fund a three-year project. My wages were secure.

We set out to answer three questions: what was it that made certain woods attractive to pheasants; how could one manage woods to make them more attractive; and what effects did this management have on other wildlife?

The first thing we did was to work out what the pheasants wanted during the winter. In Britain, there is a long history of planting woods specifically for pheasants. There are a large number of books and guides, going back to the end of the last century, describing how to make the 'ideal' pheasant covert. Despite this wealth of practical experience, however, no one had actually looked at how the birds used different areas of woodland

Pheasants fitted with small neck-mounted radio transmitters can be followed at a distance without undue disturbance.

or what precisely they needed.

We decided to go for a two-pronged approach, combining a countrywide survey of pheasant numbers in different woodland types with intensive radiotelemetry of birds in one large woodland block. The hope was that the two studies would complement each other.

RADIOTRACKING

In the 1950s and 1960s a new tool started to appear that has since revolutionised the way that many biologists study their animals: radiotelemetry. It started with large, bulky radio equipment, and there are now hundreds of different lightweight packages that can be attached to animals and allow their movements to be followed in almost any habitat and at any time of day. These have opened huge new opportunities for looking at different aspects of their behaviour, habitat selection, causes of death, mate selection and just about everything else.

The basic equipment for pheasants consists of three separate things: a small battery-powered radio transmitter that attaches to the bird and gives out a pulsed radio signal; an aerial carried by the biologist that typically gives the strongest signal when pointing towards the bird; and a receiver that turns the signal into an audible 'beep-beep' sound. The principle is simple: point the aerial towards the strongest signal to get a direction, known as a fix, repeat this from a number of different places and then triangulate to get the bird's position. Unfortunately life is never that simple. First of all, thick vegetation can block the signal and cause it to bounce, giving strong signals from all sorts of different directions. The bird can move between fixes or run away from the researcher if he gets too close, confusing the triangulation. The frequencies of the radios attached to different birds can drift during cold weather, confusing one bird with another. Worst of all, the bird can move out of the range of the aerial and it can take days of driving around the area to find it again.

Discovering the cause of death is usually one of the most important aspects of a tracking study, but finding dead birds can be one of the most difficult aspects. Foxes in particular can carry the body some distance. I have had birds taken over 2 miles before they were eaten. Foxes also have a habit of biting off the bird's head, together with the transmitter attached to the neck, and burying it separately. A radio buried under 3 or 4 inches of soil gives a signal that can only be detected within 20 yards or so. All in all, tracking pheasants generally involves walking round and round in circles for hours on end, listening to a little box going 'bleep-bleep'.

Radiotracking has its bonuses, however. It gives one a 'feel' for the birds, following them through their daily routine. The data is also extremely valuable, providing a complete life history for the bird concerned. It can also have its lighter moments: tracking birds back to poachers' houses, being accused of being a television licence inspector poking about in people's back gardens and dodging rifle shots from deer stalkers early in the morning. On most occasions one does not get to see the bird – the whole point of the technique is to follow the animal without it being bothered by one's presence. However, one sometimes gets a rare view of something really interesting. Maureen Woodburn, who has been with our pheasant team since the mid-1980s was once out on her study area on West Woodyates Farm in Dorset, following a group of hens as they were just about to start nesting. She already had a rough position on her birds and was going around them getting more accurate fixes. The last bird had been some way off when she first checked it, but when it came around to its

Tracking birds fitted with radio transmitters relies on a portable aerial to detect the signal.

turn for more detailed attention, she found that the signal was getting much closer. Looking up she saw a movement in the field and a fox running towards her. As it came closer she saw that it had a pheasant in its mouth, closer still and she could see that the bird had a radio around its neck. It was the bird she had been tracking. She followed the fox all the way back to its den.

Apart from obtaining a straightforward life history for an individual bird, tracking also enables us to collect all sorts of other information. By looking at how much time each bird spends in different habitats we can get an idea about which ones it prefers. We can recapture the same bird at almost any time to measure how its weight has changed. We can locate birds on the roost and return in the morning to collect their droppings. By sorting through the mess, we can discover their individual diets. We can also map out all of the individual fixes for a bird and use them to calculate a home range, a rough measure of the area over which it was moving. Calculating home ranges is a lengthy process in itself. There are dozens of different ways of converting a series of points on a map into an area of use, and hundreds of technical papers discussing why every other scientist has done it wrong. It is one of those situations where there is no right answer. Everyone inevitably has their own opinion and will argue their point against all comers. All in all radiotelemetry is one of our most useful tools, but the really important point is not to get bogged down in the technical details of equipment, analysis and field techniques, losing sight of the animal that was carrying the radio in the first place.

One of the big advantages of working on pheasants is that it is very simple to get people to help. During the winter, pheasants are not particularly easy to count. Luckily, British pheasant shooting relies on beaters driving birds from woodland to make them fly over the guns. All we had to do was go along to prearranged pheasant shoots and count the birds, with the beaters doing all the hard work for us. We usually ended up getting a good lunch as well. For two winters we travelled the country visiting different farms and, a day or two after the shoot, we would return to each wood and take a whole range of measurements. How big was the wood, what shape, which species of trees and shrubs, how much cover did it provide at different heights, was extra food provided, how many birds were released and what crops were grown in the surrounding fields?

By standing behind the hunters on driven pheasant shoots, we were able to count the number of birds flushed from different woodlands.

We later revisited each woodland and measured the cover provided for the birds at different heights.

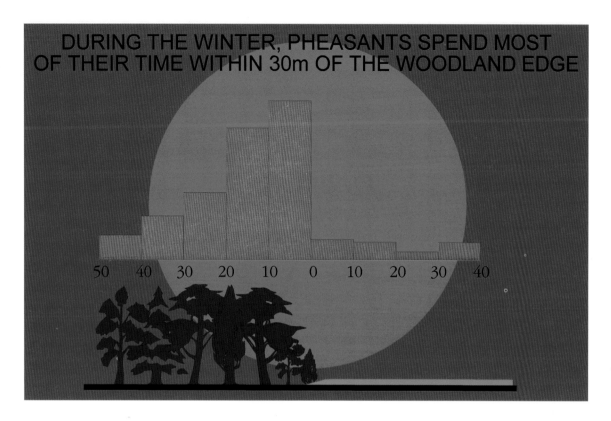

DURING THE WINTER, PHEASANTS SPEND MOST OF THEIR TIME WITHIN 30m OF THE WOODLAND EDGE

50   40   30   20   10   0   10   20   30   40

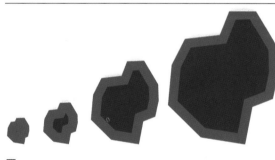

AREA RARELY USED BY PHEASANTS
AREA REGULARLY USED BY PHEASANTS
50 yds

As the size of a woodland increases, more of the area is over 50m from the edge and it will hold a lower overall density of pheasants.

We ended up with an idea of pheasant numbers and habitat characteristics from over 150 different woods, a good sample to provide an overall idea of what the birds liked. At the same time we were radiotracking birds in a large wood just outside Salisbury, following their daily movements to build up a picture of how each bird used a piece of woodland. Together, these two approaches gave us some clear insights into what sort of woods pheasants like.

The first thing is that they like small woods. From our survey of shoots we found that woods of more than 10 acres rarely held high densities of birds. The radiotracking gave us a reason for this. Birds spend the majority of their time within 30 yards of the woodland edge and rarely go more than 50 yards into a big wood. As small woods are almost all edge and very little middle, they are particularly attractive. From a management point of view this has some obvious implications. Do not plant big woods for pheasants and try to ensure that no part of the wood is more than 50 yards from open ground. In the same way, lots of edge is a good thing, so avoid square woods and go for elongated or irregular shapes.

Wide woodland rides can mimic the conditions found along woodland edges and increase the available habitat for pheasants in large blocks of woodland. (David Hill)

This is all very well when it comes to planting new woods, but what if someone already has woods but wants to improve them? What can be done in a large block to make it more attractive? As the main problem in large woods is lack of edge, we were interested to see if there were features within a wood that could mimic true woodland edges. Our radiotracking highlighted a number of areas in the middle of a large wood that were being used by the birds, in particular wide access rides. This wood contained a range of different tracks and roads, but the pheasants only seemed to use the wide ones, in particular those at least 30 yards across. It seemed that a ride of this width could mimic a true woodland edge as far as the birds were concerned, but that narrower ones could not.

Thirty-yard wide rides keep cropping up in ecological studies in woodland as having special value for wildlife. It seems that, at this width, they are wide enough for sunlight to penetrate to the ground without being shaded by the mature trees along the edge. This makes them particularly warm and allows rich vegetation to grow in the middle. So, in an existing large piece of wood, cutting these wide rides can make a big difference to the number of pheasants it will hold.

Woodland edges are obviously not the only thing that pheasants need and the next most important feature is shrubby cover. The value of shrubs for pheasants has long been appreciated. Many of the books on woodland planting for them contain long lists of plants that are thought particularly attractive. Our work certainly confirmed this. Woods with dense cover between 1 and 6 feet in height contained the most birds. As a rule of thumb, if you find it difficult to walk though a particular area of wood, it is probably a good one for pheasants. I have heard a story of a game adviser who, while training an apprentice, used to send him into a wood. He would then judge how attractive it was by the state of his assistant's clothes when he came out the other end.

One thing we did not find was any link between pheasants and particular tree or shrub species. As long as the right structure is provided at the right height, pheasants are just as happy to live in areas of young conifer, hawthorn scrub, coppiced hazel or exotic shrub species like rhododendron or lonicera (Japanese honeysuckle). It is the structure, not the species, that is important. Although some species are easier to grow, particularly some of the exotic ones, it is economics and ease of establishment that lead people to choose certain shrubs rather than any special value to the bird. I am convinced that, given proper planning, it should be possible to make attractive pheasant habitat out of old car bodies and cardboard boxes; the only problem has been to find someone willing to try it on a large scale!

Saying that shrubs are important is one thing, accurately describing the value of different types of cover is another. Scientists are very fond of calculating equations to describe these sorts of things. However, we wanted something simple that we could show to forest managers to give them a clear visual impression of what we were talking about. Starting with our figures on the cover in all the different woods, we worked out a simple index of attractiveness. This ranked different woods from very poor to near perfection in terms of the cover they provided. Starting at zero for an area without a single piece of cover of any sort (we actually took some measurements of a car park outside a supermarket) through to scores of around 50 for some of the best bits of cover we saw, we were able to present pictures of different woods together with numbers indicating their attractiveness. The numbers do not actually mean that a particular wood will hold a certain number of pheasants – that obviously depends on a whole range of other things apart from just shrubby cover. What they do show is that, everything else being equal, a wood with a score of 20 for shrubby cover should hold twice as many birds as one with an index of ten. (see pictures on page 28)

Creating the right sort of shrubby cover is no easy business; it requires considerable forethought and planning. With existing woods, the most common problem is that the tree canopy is complete and any shrubs present in the understorey are shaded and straggly. Planting new shrubs in these circumstances is no answer; the important thing is to let more light into the wood by clearing or thinning the canopy. This should allow the existing shrubs to flourish or, if they are really thin on the ground, newly planted shrubs to thrive. As pheasants are particularly attracted to the woodland edge this is the first part of a wood that should be considered. In many cases existing woodland edges are shaded by tall trees, suppressing shrub growth in just the same way as in the middle. The trees often also shade the farmer's crop in the neighbouring field, so cutting back the overhanging standard trees can benefit both game and agriculture. At first sight, the results of all this cutting can be very ugly, turning what was originally a moderately attractive area into something bare and open to the wind. However, given a few years it will regrow into ideal pheasant habitat, so a planned rotation of management is best, to ensure that there is a mixture of newly cut, ideal and ageing plots in any one area.

A bare and shaded woodland edge such as this provides little benefit for pheasants. (The Game Conservancy)

We calculated indices of the attractiveness of different woodland types to pheasants based on the cover they provide.

Mature Beech

Thinned Pine

Old Hazel Coppice

Young Larch and Birch

Rhododendron

Coppiced Hazel

Woodland edges well supplied with shrubby cover provide ideal pheasant habitat during both winter and spring. (Mike Swan)

A problem regularly encountered in some areas is livestock grazing in woodland. The best way to ruin a piece of pheasant cover is to let the cattle or sheep in. Many of the woods I have seen, particularly in Ireland and parts of North America, have been spoiled in this way. In these cases fencing is the best answer, allowing shrubs to regenerate once the offending animals are excluded. Small woods are often valued by farmers as providing shelter for their stock; to avoid conflict it is not necessary to fence the entire wood; increasing the shrubs in just part of the wood may be enough and could also increase the shelter for livestock where wind and rain are a problem.

In new woodlands there is obviously much more opportunity to lay the area out in an attractive way. In Britain, government subsidies for

One method of improving the attractiveness of newly planted woodlands, known as the instant spinney, is to interplant a game crop between the rows of trees.

29

new woodland planting are subject to the condition that the area should contain a high proportion of tall timber trees. These can easily be incorporated into the designs but are not really essential, or even desirable, if the primary aim is to create pheasant cover. A typical planting design for British woodland includes a dense hedgerow around the edge, rising through medium-height timber species to the full standard trees. The concentration of shrubs at the woodland edge ensures that the area will be windproof once it is established, while setting the tall tree species back from the edge means that they will not overhang and shade the edge once they are well grown. It is also important to include a proportion of shrubs within the body of the wood at the time of planting, allowing them to become firmly established before the canopy closes.

It takes time for a new piece of cover to become established and attractive to the birds. The wait for an expensive new planting to start holding birds can be very frustrating. There are a number of ways of speeding things up, or at least providing some interim cover in the early years. Two popular options include planting a high proportion of conifers at the start. These can be very attractive to pheasants in their early years, well before most broadleaved species. However, most of the conifers should be removed once the broadleaves begin to become attractive in their own right. Young conifers can be heaven to pheasants but, if they grow too old they can be among the worst trees for them. It is worth leaving a few clumps of conifers to grow on to maturity – say 5 per cent of the total area planted – as they can be very popular for roosting. It is also possible to keep conifers attractive by cutting them off at waist height if they start to become thin at the bottom. This is sacrilege to most foresters, but it can work quite well.

The second way of speeding up the attractiveness of a new planting is to sow a game crop between the rows of trees. These can provide good cover for the first few years when the trees are small, and they are eventually shaded out as the trees develop. Combined with an inclusion of fast-growing conifers this can ensure pheasant cover throughout the life of a wood. This approach has been particularly popular in Britain, where landowners often like to see rapid results from their investment in new woods. The inclu-sion of game crops within newly established woodlands, instant spinneys as they are known, has formed a large proportion of the new small farm woodlands established in recent years. By combining the early cover provided by the crops, the secondary benefits of conifers and then the long-term advantages of a mixed shrub and broadleaved tree plantation it has been possible to provide a well-rounded and popular method of planting winter covers. Shrubby cover is the key and instant spinneys use the options to good advantage.

The best shrub species vary considerably around the world and depend more on what will grow in a particular area than anything else. Hawthorn is a popular shrub in southern England; the Duke of Argyll's tea plant works in Austria; sea buckthorn is ideal in some northern regions of China; dogwoods, plum, choke-cherry and multiflora rose (an unpopular choice with local farmers) are good in parts of North America. The lists and variations are endless. The key is to find a species that grows to about 5 or 6 feet in height, maintains a bushy growth form throughout its life and is sufficiently dense near ground level. One trick of game advisers when visiting a new area, and one I have used to good effect myself, is to keep an eye open for the best areas of cover during an introductory tour of the land. If you see a particularly good clump of a particular species, say privet, occurring naturally on the farm, a comment on the lines of 'Privet might do well on this land' can often sound impressive. This is especially good when the owner replies, 'Yes, you're right, I have a good privet patch on the edge of the wood we passed an hour ago.' The best way of deciding what shrub to plant is not to read 'how to plant pheasant cover' books, but to have a mental picture of the sort of things the birds are looking for and to then see what grows best in your own locality.

After edges and shrubs, the next most important factor in making a wood attractive to pheasants is food. Our work was mainly based on woods where birds were intensively managed for driven shooting, and in most cases grain was supplied by the gamekeepers to meet the birds requirements. Not surprisingly, the more food was provided, the more pheasants we found. The wood had to be the right size and shape as well as having good shrubs, but the amount of supplementary feeding had a significant effect. In Britain, food is typically provided in three ways: by daily spreading grain onto woodland rides, by setting feed hoppers throughout a wood, or by planting a food crop, typically maize, nearby. Britain is fairly atypical when it comes to the intensity of pheasant management and in most other countries the birds have to subsist on natural or occasional food sources. Berried shrubs can help, but I think their importance is often very overrated. Waste grain, silage heaps and weed seeds are far more important. To a large extent the availability of these food sources depends on the farmer. In intensively farmed areas or where deep snow hides the food from the birds, it is better to provide either maize food crops or grain in hoppers. Forget seed-bearing shrubs; too many other birds feed on them as well, and the seeds are usually gone by the time things get really hard. For those who still want to pursue them, however, an early Game Conservancy study found that sea buckthorn berries were the birds' favourite, and they were certainly very abundant in the best wild pheasant area I saw in China. They also make a nice laxative soup!

It is worth pointing out that our study was largely based on areas where birds had been released the previous summer. Obviously, the number of birds we counted was heavily influenced by the extent of rearing. I have made a point of not referring to actual numbers of birds in a piece of cover, concentrating on why some woods are more attractive than others. Releasing birds can increase the total number in an area, but it will not change the fact that some woods are more attractive than others. Even reared birds are pretty good at choosing winter covers, and if they are released into the wrong area they will quickly move somewhere more attractive.

Looking back, I think there are a few things we missed when we did this work. None of them are particularly easy to quantify, but they could be important nevertheless. I think that one of the main reasons pheasants like scrub is that it gives them three things: escape cover from predators, ease of movement at ground level and protection from the weather. The importance of these three factors varies between different areas. In North America, there are a whole range of large predatory birds – red-tailed hawks and great horned owls spring immediately to mind – that can be important predators of pheasants during the winter. Both species choose tall trees as perches and, quite sensibly, pheasants in these areas seem to avoid pieces of cover near them. I still think that the British approach to shrubs is relevant to North America, but many of our designs for pheasant coverts have too many tall trees to make sense there.

Protection from the weather is another factor which varies in importance between different areas, and it can be provided by other things apart from shrubs. In southern England, the weather that the birds are trying to avoid is cold wind, and woods surrounded by earth banks or containing pits seem to hold more birds as they are effectively wind-proofed. But our studies did not take account of the ability of the birds to survive and in fact thrive in areas with no trees or shrubs at all. For someone used to seeing pheasants spending the winter in woodland it can come as a considerable shock to visit an area where marshland or ditches provide the main winter covers, and I know the same is true in reverse. Once, when I described to an American hunter how British pheasants spend the winter in woodland, he said, 'Are you sure we are talking about the same bird?'

My first experience of this difference came on a visit to the fens of East Anglia. I had heard of the good wild pheasant populations in this part of the country and an invitation to watch a shoot was my first opportunity to see how they thrived. These areas on the east coast of Britain were reclaimed from the sea and are criss-crossed by an extensive network of ditches and dykes. They also contain some of the best wild pheasant populations in the country. At first I found it hard to believe we would see any pheasants at all. Apart from a few trees around the farm buildings the whole area seemed bare of any cover. Having been reclaimed from the sea it was also incredibly flat. The highest point on the farm was only a few feet above sea level and the cold easterly winds from Russia blew uninterrupted across the landscape. However, I watched in surprise as the pheasants appeared from apparently nowhere, the beaters flushing large numbers of birds from the ditches and stubble fields. Despite the exposed nature of the fens, the birds very

Many different species of shrub can provide good pheasant cover, ranging from sea buckthorn in China (below) to regrowing hazel in an English woodland (above). The important thing is the height and density of the plant, not the individual species concerned.

Berries are often a favoured food item, as with this sea buckthorn bush in China, but their importance is often overestimated.

In many open areas, such as the fenlands of eastern England, ditches and reedy areas can provide the only suitable winter pheasant cover. (above)

In Britain, game crops such as kale are often used to supplement woodland as winter cover. They can also be an important part of the design of driven shoots. Note the game crop on the opposite hillside.

happily spend the winters in reed-filled ditches, warmly protected from the wind.

The same is true in many parts of North America, where cattail marshes, stubbles and tussock grasses can be the main forms of winter cover. Marshlands are the main wintering areas for pheasants in many parts of North America and should not be underestimated. Extensive cattail stands can provide superb wintering cover and often contain clumps of shrub as well. More importantly they are also areas where farmers are willing to tolerate habitat management as they do not impact on their crops.

Woods are certainly the main wintering areas in Britain and many other parts of the world, but they are clearly not the only habitats that pheasants will use. Even in wooded areas, they will spend much of their time in various cover crops, kale, maize, mustard and a variety of other crops can provide good cover for them. These can be particularly effective if placed next to an existing wood or if they are well supplied with feeding sites; the birds move from their roosts in the woods to the cover crops on a daily basis. This is something that is often exploited on British driven pheasant shoots. The birds are enticed from the woods to carefully sited game crops and then driven back home to their roosting sites to provide challenging targets for the hunters.

Game crops can certainly provide a cheap and simple way of supplementing winter cover in Britain. However, as the winter proceeds and frosts gradually thin out the crops, they become less and less attractive and the birds spend more time in the woods. They are also tied quite closely to the woods. Game crops are fine as feeding areas during the day but British birds prefer to roost in trees and will make woodland their home at night. During our winter radiotracking we never found a pheasant that roosted on the ground. In every case they roosted up trees and seemed to prefer dense, fairly windproof sites with lots of side branches. Unthinned larch and spruce plantations seemed particularly good, although some birds also roosted in dense hawthorn scrub and overgrown hazel. The main idea seemed to be to find somewhere warm and off the ground. Particularly good roosts can attract large numbers of birds. On one of our study areas, a 3 acre larch plantation was the most popular roost I have found. It was a dense unthinned plot, about 25 feet tall. Apart from about 3 feet of open ground at the bottom it was extremely dense and almost impenetrable. I have sat and watched 200–300 pheasants congregate at dusk on a track that runs along one side of the plot, eventually flying up into the branches in small groups, cackling and crowing as they settled down for the night.

Even where there are woods, pheasants do not always seem to go for the same sorts of roost sites. Karl Pock, an Austrian gamekeeper, once showed me his birds at roost. Rather than concentrating in the middle of dense windproof areas, his birds seemed to like perching singly on the very tips of tall, spindly pseudo-acacia trees. They must have had almost no protection from the wind and with a torch we could see them clearly silhouetted against the sky. Karl's view was that this was the only place they could feel secure from stone martens, which are adept at climbing trees at night and certainly capable of taking pheasants. So pheasants choose their roost sites as protection from predators as well as the wind.

British pheasants will certainly roost on the ground if they have no choice. As I have said, in the treeless fenlands of East Anglia they choose to spend the nights in reed-filled ditches or long-standing stubbles. But even here they will go for trees if they are introduced. One farmer I know planted a small, dense woodland for his birds. Once it had grown it filled up each night with pheasants from the surrounding lands, which concentrated in the trees to roost.

In many parts of North America the birds seem less fond of roosting up trees and most studies refer to birds spending the nights on the ground, even when trees are available. It is not that North American pheasants never roost up trees; John Carroll has a collection of anecdotes relating to tree roosting by pheasants from Massachusetts to South Dakota, but the fact remains that it is not considered the norm. One time when many of them do choose trees is in dense snow cover. I once described the tree-roosting habits of British pheasants to George Wilson, a Utah game warden, and the only local case he could think of was three cocks that spent three days up a tree after a blizzard. John Carroll also remembers a photograph from Massachusetts of a cock hanging by its tail from a tree after a freezing rain storm.

If British fenland birds only roost on the ground when they have no choice, why should their American cousins so often shun trees? The only thing I can think of is that roosting up trees in North America is more dangerous than sitting on the ground, possibly because of the large owls and other birds of prey that are found in such abundance. It cannot be a genetic difference, as the American pheasants originate from European and Chinese birds and in both these areas they regularly roost up trees. My guess is that roost site selection is driven by the risk of predation. British birds roost up trees because the main predator they have to worry about is the red fox. Austrian birds choose exposed trees to avoid the added danger of stone martens. North American pheasants have a whole range of different predators to worry about, including big night-hunting birds of prey. On balance they seem to have decided that the ground predators are the lesser risk. The only exception is when there is dense snow cover, when it may be particularly easy to find them on the ground.

For much of the winter the birds form flocks; it is the time of year when cover and food are in greatest shortage and the birds are at their most tolerant of each other. In Britain, however, where winter cover is fairly abundant, the cocks and hens choose to live in separate flocks. The two sexes do not actually avoid each other, but when we have looked at the numbers of males and females found together in winter, we have discovered that they mix a lot less than we would expect. Typically we find large flocks of hens congregating in the warmest, best-supplied and most secure areas. Some of the cocks live there as well and will hang around with the hens, but many form small flocks in outlying pieces of habitat. It is not that the sexes do not mix, just that the hens seem to form larger groups than the males.

When we were starting our work on winter habitats, David Hill and I heard some accounts of cock and hen pheasants preferring different woods. Our initial studies of reared pheasants found little evidence for this; both sexes seemed to like exactly the same sorts of woods. However, I have now had the chance to see many more wild populations during the winter and I do think there is some truth in these accounts. It is not that there are some woods for hens and some for cocks, rather that most woods hold good numbers of both while others only seem to contain males. This is only really apparent in wild pheasant areas, presumably because the extensive feeding that goes on on reared pheasant shoots masks the effect.

What I think is happening is that the females are very tolerant of each other during the winter and form large flocks in the best bits of habitat. Although the males also concentrate in the best areas, they are more aggressive towards each other and do not form large flocks except in particularly hard weather. This means that they tend to spread out into other, less attractive areas. Presumably the young or sub-dominant birds are excluded from the best woods. Certain woods, which are not attractive enough to draw a large flock of hens, may still be good enough for some of these males. I have been to two wild shoots where, in amongst groups of warm and secure woodlands, there were a small number of less attractive and on the shoot days draughty ones. In each case my hosts said that these woods only seemed to hold cocks. It is not real evidence but it makes sense. From a management viewpoint it is also quite useful. A wood that only holds cocks is one that needs work. It is not good enough to attract the fussy hens and can only hold the males excluded from the best areas. However, it is not so bad that no pheasants will use it and, with a little work, it could be considerably improved. The presence of a disproportionate number of males is a handy way of picking those woods that should show the most improvement for the least work.

Why should the cocks spread themselves out while the hens concentrate in the best spots? I think it is a mixture of two reasons. First, the cocks are beginning to lay claim to potential territory sites and spread themselves out to be ready to start in the spring. This leads on to the second reason, that dominant males do not like having too many competitors around, so young or weak cocks are forced to live away from the best sites. As the best winter habitats also form the best territories, this means that sub-dominant males are squeezed out.

Cock pheasants are certainly aggressive in late autumn. Many of the displays that they use in the breeding season can also be seen, in a watered down form, in autumn. They will go through a

During the winter, pheasants form loose flocks. Although the sexes will mix they tend to segregate into large female flocks and smaller, less stable male groups.

Hen pheasants seem to be fussier than the males and will spend the winter in the best pieces of available cover. (David Hill)

During the winter the dominant males start to lay claim to the best territory sites and sub-dominant males are forced to live in less suitable habitats.

Prolonged snow cover can be a major killer of pheasants in many parts of America. This melanistic hen in England has little to worry about in this regard.

variety of head-bobbing displays, crow and even fight. It has been said that this was just because their hormones were confused. Sexual hormones such as testosterone are, to some extent, controlled by day length in pheasants. When the days start getting longer and there is more sunlight in spring, this seems to trigger their release and the start of mating behaviour. The theory is that, when the whole thing happens in reverse in autumn it could trigger a similar effect. I do not think that there is much truth in this, however. I believe aggressive behaviour amongst cocks in autumn has a real function. They are sorting out their pecking order for the coming winter, with the dominant birds getting the best spots near to their spring territories.

This sort of sexual segregation, with the hens concentrated and the cocks spread out, seems to work well in Britain, where the winters are mild and there is no real shortage of cover. However, in parts of the American Midwest, winter storms can be a real killer and winter cover is hard to find. A Hampshire pheasant sitting out an English rainstorm in a dense thicket is pampered compared to an Illinois bird trying to hide from driving snow in a patch of long stubble. In many areas like this, there just is not enough winter cover for the cocks to space themselves out; shortage of cover and extreme weather force them and hens to flock together. As with so many aspects of their lives, the birds adapt to local conditions. It is not that they want different things, just that what is possible varies from place to place.

Extreme winter weather, particularly pro-longed snow, can kill large numbers of birds, and it is very easy to see such conditions as something that managers can do little about. This is espe-cially a problem in parts of North America, where deep snow can lie for months on end and fine driving snow can swamp birds and freeze on their bodies. In conditions like this, death seems to come in three ways: direct chilling or being buried; starvation; or increased predation. In each case it is possible to think of ways to reduce the problem. But the scale of the problem can be very large indeed; the late John Gates, a biologist in Wisconsin, lost 80 per cent of his birds in the hard winter of 1961–2, and American hunters are full of horror stories about the conditions they, and the birds, have had to endure, with hands frozen

to shotguns and birds found with balls of ice formed over their mouths. Losses from extreme winter weather can be heavy indeed.

How can the effects of prolonged or driving snow be overcome? Let us take take each of the causes of death in turn. Direct freezing or burying seems to be most prevalent in the wide open plains. In these areas drifting snow is a real menace and the winter cover for the birds is usually only reedy cattail areas or tall standing grasses. Creating patches of dense shrub should both reduce the chances of drifts covering any birds that are using them and provide warm, wind-sheltered conditions. (Planting shrubs in these open areas may also hold the key to increasing spring breeding populations, but for quite a different reason, as discussed later.) If the birds are dying of exposure, give them something to hide behind!

The second problem is starvation. Deep or fine blowing snow can quickly cover any food and make it hard for the birds to get at it, but there is more to the problem than that. In very cold weather, when energy loss from chilling is high, it may pay the birds to give up feeding. They may lose more energy trying to find a little food than they would just sitting tight. This certainly seems to happen; in Finland, birds have been found to conserve energy by remaining still and torpid for days on end. During an unusually cold spell in Britain, Matt Ridley, a British scientist of whom I shall say more later, found that his birds stayed on the roost for almost a week and did not attempt to feed. Pheasants can withstand quite long periods without food, up to about 16 days at between -4 and $-15°C$. They survive on their reserves of body fat. Birds found dead during such weather seem to have reached the end of their reserves and are often 50–60 per cent lighter than before the storms. The policy of 'sit and wait' cannot work for ever and in really long periods of cold the birds have no choice but to look for food. The crops of such birds are usually empty. Internal bleeding, from eating very coarse food is not uncommon, nor is cannibalism, at least when it comes to eating earlier victims of the same conditions. If the birds are dying from lack of food because it is covered, or they will not venture away from the relative warmth of the roost to look for it, then the obvious solution is to give them food near the roost. Feed hoppers in the warmest spots, raised up on bricks if the snow is likely to be deep, are an obvious solution, as are food crops next to the best roosts if these can be kept free of drifts by careful siting. The important thing is to feed them right next to the roost and to keep the feeding site as sheltered as possible.

The last problem is predation. It is no coincidence that hen pheasants are coloured to look like dead grass, as camouflage is an important way of avoiding predators. However, this does not work well in snow, especially when they are already weak and are leaving a trail of footprints behind them. The effects of snow can be dramatic. A Wisconsin study radiotracked birds throughout the year to get an idea of the timing and causes of losses. In a typical week, a stock of 1,000 birds would lose 10 or 20 of its members, usually to a mammalian predator. During nesting, normally considered one of the most dangerous periods for the birds, the weekly losses might rise to 30 or 40 birds per thousand. However, when snow was lying, the rate rose to 50–70 birds per week. There was an especially high loss to birds of prey making easy kills on weak birds standing out against the white background. Losses to mammals did not seem any worse in snow; it was the birds of prey that made the difference.

I have seen just the sort of conditions that can contribute to this. I visited Utah in early 1993 when the snow was about 1 foot deep. The temperature was quite mild and the birds were able to look for food without worrying about chilling. I was taken to see a particularly good farm on the edge of a large wetland where many of the local birds had congregated in the dense willow scrub on some of the islands. The main food source for these birds was the silage pit in the farmyard, the better part of a mile from the willow scrub. Every morning the birds had to trek across the snow from the cover to the pit, fill up with food and then run the gauntlet home again – ideal conditions for any flying predator. At the other end of the farm, the local Pheasants Forever chapter had set up a series of feed hoppers along the edge of the wetland. Here the birds could hop back and forward from their roosts to the food with hardly a vulnerable moment. The principles for decreasing deaths from exposure or starvation apply to predation as well. If the birds have what they need in a small, secure area they will not

need to expose themselves to the risks of predation.

The decimating effects of cold winters are mainly a North American condition. Such intense weather is rare in western Europe and we still know too little about China to assess the way the birds react there. However, this simple example of how the importance of weather can be reduced by giving the birds something to hide behind and ensuring that the food is nearby, puts paid to the idea that death from bad weather is simply an Act of God.

Well-sited food hoppers near to secure winter cover, as with this one in Utah, can help reduce losses to starvation and predation.

Spring sees the onset of territorial behaviour in pheasants.

TERRITORIES

Every year I look forward to April, in my opinion the best month of the year. It is not just that everything is starting to grow and the British weather is starting to become a little less wet. It is also the time when the pheasants are at their most interesting. By April the cocks have set up their territories and spend a lot of time displaying. They seem to have more character in April than in the whole of the rest of the year put together. From being skulking and secretive during the winter, all of a sudden they emerge in the full glory of their plumage and strut around for all the world to see.

Each year a cock would set up his territory in my back garden, and soon became fairly used to us being around. This was especially true once my son was old enough to run around the garden. After being chased by him a few times, they soon realised that we were no threat and were quite content to have us around. It was a real pleasure to see the cock going through his displays every morning as I left for work, and many of the photographs in this book were taken out of the windows of the house. However, it is all too easy to see the birds as just quaint, their displays and behaviour as nothing more than a curiosity to brighten up a spring morning. From the birds' point of view it is one of the most

Pheasants are unusual birds in that one male will try to attract a group of females to breed with him on his territory.

dangerous and violent times of year. Their displays all have real and important purposes, telling us a great deal about what the birds need and what is important to them. The sights that brightened my April mornings were a matter of life and death to the birds themselves

Pheasants are unusual birds in many ways, and one of the most obvious is the way they organise themselves during the breeding season. Their habit of one male breeding with numerous females which remain with him on his territory is extremely unusual in birds, but it has not always endeared them to people. Viscount Grey of Fallodon, the famous ornithologist of the early twentieth century, who gave his name to the Edward Grey Institute of Field Ornithology at Oxford, was certainly not impressed. In his book, *The Charm of Birds*, he launched a diatribe against what he saw as their degenerate behaviour: 'British birds are monogamous; this is the rule and the exceptions are few . . . Pheasants are not indigenous . . . They need not be taken into account; the inferiority of their habits is not native to Britain, and our country is not responsible for them.'

The Edward Grey Institute has long been a centre of excellence for bird studies and has, incidentally, been the source of many projects which have overturned Grey's statement that British birds are monogamous. As it turns out many of our common species are not averse to a bit of mixed mating. It was also there that Matt Ridley carried out a three-year study into the mating system of the pheasant. Before his work, much of the information we had on pheasant breeding behaviour dealt simply with *what* they did – descriptions of displays etc. – rather than asking *why*. His thesis was much more questioning and, by identifying what makes pheasants breed in such an unusual way, gave some valuable insights into their management.

ESTABLISHING TERRITORIES

In the spring the males set up territories. These areas are typically established on the edges of cover where they border on open ground. A male lays claim to an area and goes through a range of displays to deter intruders, only resorting to actual violence on rare occasions. Once he has his terri-

tory he goes through a further series of displays to attract females, the most obvious of which is crowing. While this is going on, the females are still in their winter flocks, and they tour an area assessing the qualities of each of the males. Eventually they choose one to settle with and join his harem. They then remain with him for about a month before leaving to incubate their nest. While with the male they emerge from the cover each morning and evening to feed at his feet while he stands guard over them. This system is known as territorial harem defence polygyny and is extremely rare in birds, although quite common in mammals. Why do they do this? I am sure it is not random or just some peculiarity of pheasants, there must be very good reasons why they breed in this way. To understand what goes on during the early spring it is best to look at the sexes separately; they behave very differently and are looking for different things.

All through the winter the males are spread out through the cover, sometimes joining the flocks of hens or associating with other males, but rarely forming any lasting groups. They establish their own pecking order; it seems that a lot of the competition for dominance goes on during the winter although the birds rarely fight. In Britain, with its abundance of small woods and other sorts of cover for our mild winters, the males are able to stay relatively close to where they hope to establish their territories in the spring. This is probably one of the reasons why the cocks are intolerant of each other during the winter. They are already trying to lay claim to suitable areas for their territories and the best winter covers seem to make the best territories as well. In February, when territory formation really gets under way, the old, dominant males rarely move far from their winter ranges, while younger birds have to move further afield. Matt Ridley found that adult cocks which had already held a territory in a previous year only moved an average of 75 yards from their winter ranges to their territories. This compares with 250 yards for birds holding a territory for the first time and 350 yards for males which fail to get a territory and remain non-territorial.

Where then are the territories established? There have been a large number of studies looking at this and they all reach broadly similar conclusions. Cock pheasants start to set up their territories in February or March, usually on the edge of some form of cover, where it borders on open ground. The sort of cover used varies around the world, but the principle is the same. Whether they go for hawthorn scrub at the edges of woodland in southern England, strips of bankside willow in Utah, reed-filled ditches in eastern England, tall, standing grasses in Kansas or bamboo in China, they are all looking for the same thing. The prime requisite seems to be some form of cover that they can hide in during the day, right next to a piece of open ground where they can feed on the growing crops, grasses or seeds left over from the previous year. These two things are what make up a territory: a combination of somewhere dense to hide and somewhere open to feed. Why this arrangement of food and cover is important is something I will return to later.

Once a cock has set up a territory, he obviously has to defend it against other males. Matt Ridley, and other scientists before him, identified a series of displays that territory-holders used to deter other males which wandered into his area. The simplest display was for the territory-holder to walk towards the intruder with his head and tail held high – the 'walk threat'. In most cases the intruder then crouched and, as the territory-holder came closer, either fled or adopted a submissive posture with the feathers on the top of his head raised. If the intruder stood his ground then the territory-holder moved on to the next display. This 'peck threat' involved the territorial bird pecking at the ground near to the intruder.

In most cases these relatively simple displays led to the intruder breaking off the challenge and fleeing the territory. If he decided to stay, the territorial bird moved on to a more threatening display, the 'lateral strut'. In this he moved slowly in front of his rival with his tail feathers spread and one wing drooping, apparently designed to make his body seem as large as possible. This display almost always led to the intruder giving up his challenge. If not the territory owner would turn on the other and attack him, which resulted in the intruder flying off, closely followed by the territorial male in an 'aerial chase'.

For almost all of the male to male displays that Matt observed, the territory owner ended up the winner. The only times he lost was when he was a young bird and it was early in the season, when

Walk threat

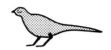

Dominant male has large wattles and erect ear-tufts, body feathers fluffed up

Sub-dominant male has small wattles, no ear-tufts, sleek body feathers

Lateral strut

Dominant male has large wattles and erect ear tufts. Wing drooping and tail fanned to make body look as large as possible, feathers at base of tail fanned out

Sub-dominant male has small wattles, no ear-tufts, sleek body feathers

Fight

Dominant male has wattles and ear-tufts, body feathers sleek, tail raised, under-tail feathers fluffed-up

Sub-dominant male also has large wattles and erect ear-tufts

43

Pheasant territories seem to contain a mixture of dense cover for concealment and open ground for feeding and display.

The sight and sound of a crowing cock pheasant is one of the most distinctive features of the spring, but what is the function of this behaviour? (Alexis de la Serre)

Once the hens emerge, the cocks stop crowing and stand alert while the hens feed.

the territory boundaries were still being defined. The displays also escalated from the non-violent 'walk threat' through the intimidating 'peck threat' and 'lateral strut' to the violent 'aerial chase'. In most cases the intruder left before actual violence ensued. The earlier displays convinced him that the territory owner was not to be played with and territory owners very rarely lost to a challenger once their territories were established.

Pheasants will of course fight, but usually when two birds are disputing the boundaries of their territories or when rivals battle over the owner-ship of a new territory from which the old owner has disappeared. True fights are also ritualised. They start with the birds crouching and facing each other; periodically one bird leaps into the air and attacks the other with his feet and spurs. These fights usually last about 15 minutes but can go on for over an hour. Disputes between two territory-holders usually result in a draw, the birds walking parallel to each other along the newly settled boundary. But fights between two non-territorial males over ownership of a vacant territory can become very violent. In these, the winner will often chase the defeated bird after the result has been decided, trying to catch his tail feathers in a prolonged chase, and breaking them if at all possible. The winners of these fights become the owners of the new territories, and the losers can be seriously injured or even killed.

Of course, it is not always true that territorial birds always win these disputes. It is perhaps better to say that the winner of a challenge, unless it is a border dispute between two neighbouring territories, usually goes on to hold the territory, and the winner is *usually* the one who has already established a claim to the territory. But territories can also change hands halfway through the season. In my first spring of field work on Lyons Estate in Ireland I tagged all the cocks in the main part of my study area and got to know most of them fairly well. One cock in particular, tagged 'C1', was a real character. He had been befriended by one of the stable lads on the estate at quite a young age. Every morning he would appear in the yard for a handful of oats and he soon became the biggest, glossiest bird in the area. When the breeding season came, C1 quickly set about all the other cocks in the area and established a territory on the edge of the estate's lake. He aggressively kept three other non-territorial males away from his ground and attracted a harem of three hens. However, he also had a couple of eccentricities. First, he would spend hours displaying to himself in the plate glass windows of one of the offices. He would also attack any humans who tried to walk through his territory. The ladies from the estate canteen were especially prone to his attentions, although I never worked out whether he saw them as rivals or potential mates; they ran back to the canteen whenever he jumped out of the bushes. With a bit of practice I found that I could get him to perform the full sequence of aggressive displays to me if I stood my ground and uttered threatening clucks back to him. From giving the 'walk threat' when I first appeared, he would quickly follow with the 'peck threat' and then the 'lateral strut' when I failed to turn and run. I found I could not do the 'lateral strut' very easily, but by flicking leaves towards him I gave a passable imitation of the 'peck threat'. This drove him mad and he would lunge up my leg, clawing my trousers and trying to spur me.

I think he wore himself out with these constant displays to everyone who went past, as his territory was on a favourite path for the estate workers. One day in mid-April a colleague rushed in to my office to say that he had seen all three of the non-territorial birds taking it in turns to fight poor C1, and that the last of them had finally routed him and pulled out his tail. I went to look for him and found him huddled under a bush at the edge of his old territory, while the winner of the battles was busy displaying to his erstwhile harem. The hens eventually took a dislike to the newcomer and joined the harem of another nearby male, but the unfortunate C1's days of chasing the canteen ladies were over. He never got over the shock and was taken by a fox four days after losing his territory.

While these male to male displays are dramatic, the most obvious part of a cock's territorial behaviour is his call. A crowing male pheasant is one of the most familiar sounds of the countryside. At dawn or dusk in spring these characteristic calls carry for miles and, for me at least, are the clear sign that the winter is over. Why do they do it? The two reasons that make most sense are to call up the hens and to deter other males. Whatever the reason they certainly put their hearts into it. The crow itself is a surprisingly loud and throaty 'kok-kok', followed by an energetic wing-drum that can only be heard at close quarters. With practice it is possible to identify individual males by their crow; each is slightly different and they range from deep resonant booming to strangled screeches.

In 1992 a student from Oxford, Mark Winterbottom, came to work with us for a six-week project and he uncovered some surprising facts about pheasant crowing and why they do it. Things did not start well for him, as a wet, cold spring delayed the crowing season and he cooled his heels for the first few weeks. A fine spell in April made up for it, however, and he spent each morning and evening listening to a group of birds on one of our study farms. We had already marked most of the birds in the area and he was able to say how often each bird crowed, which other birds were nearby when it did and how many hens were in the male's harem.

The first thing he discovered was that the males crow fastest in the morning before the hens come out to join them, and that some males crow much more often than others. Once the hens come out to feed, all this changes. The males which crow the fastest to start with tend to be the ones with the most hens, but when the hens are there they more or less stop crowing and stand quietly on guard. Cocks with no hens or only a few keep on crowing even when the hens are out. This makes sense if crowing is a way of advertising to the hens. The fact that the calls carry so far also suggests that they are sending messages over some distance, not just to the cock next door. After the male has enough hens to keep him busy he slows down and spends his time looking after his harem. This suggests that crowing is not a way of keeping other males out of the territory. If that were the case they would keep crowing when the hens are out feeding, the time when other cocks would be most tempted to interfere. It seems as though crowing is primarily a way of attracting hens, a loud and individually distinctive advertisement of the cock's health and vigour. It is even possible that the males interfere with each other's calls. Matt Ridley observed that sometimes a male will give a high-pitched call in the middle of one of his neighbour's crows, possibly to confuse the hens and upset the message he is trying to convey.

THE COCK'S HAREM

For the cocks, March and April are busy months, but for the hens things are rather different. They spend most of the winter in flocks, safe in the best areas of cover. In late February and March they start to move away from these areas and look for a suitable mate. While the cocks are busy setting up their territories, the hens remain in large flocks. They will visit a number of different territories early in the season before deciding which cock to settle with. Watching how the groups of birds change during late March and early April is very illuminating. Matt Ridley found a very rapid change over this period. While in March most hens are in flocks of four to six birds and only about 40 per cent of them are accompanied by cocks, in April this changes. The hen groups are now smaller, about three hens on average, and 90 per cent are seen with a cock. Late March and early April are obviously when the hen flocks break up and they settle with their chosen males. The hens also move further from their winter quarters than the males. An average male moves 200 yards from his winter range to his territory, typical females move over 300 yards. Interestingly, early April is when the first matings are usually seen. It seems therefore as though the hens spend March eyeing up the available males, and April actually getting on with the process of mating.

The cocks use a number of distinct behaviours to attract hens to their harems. Crowing and posturing on their territories certainly give the hens their first clue as to the male's attractiveness. But during late March and early April, when most hens are deciding whom to settle with, the cocks start to use a particular set of displays. The cock will walk towards a group of hens with his wattles and ear-tufts fully erect, the 'ritual approach', allowing the hens to get a good look at him. If a lone female approaches a territorial male he may then start what is known as the 'lateral display'. This is very similar to the 'lateral strut' that cocks

use to intimidate their rivals, spreading the tail and drooping one wing towards the hen to make the body look as large as possible. The function of this behaviour is probably very similar to that of human males flexing their muscles on a beach – to impress the girls and deter competitors. From Matt's studies of marked birds it seems as though the 'lateral display' is only given to strange hens on their own, and is an enticement to come and settle with that male.

Once a male has attracted a hen to his harem he uses a different set of displays, in particular 'tid-bitting', where he holds his head low and partly to one side, calling the female to an item of food that he points to with his beak. This display only seems to be given to hens that are regular members of his harem. These same hens also 'invite' the territory owner to mate, typically by squatting down in front of him with their tails raised. It appears, therefore, that females volunteer to mate with the male to whose harem they belong.

All of this suggests that cock and hen pheasants establish a bond during the breeding season. The hens spend between four and six weeks in the company of one male, they instigate copulation with him and resist unsolicited matings from strangers – 'forced copulation' attempts. The males also give different displays to strange hens and ones which are already in their harem. Lastly, when both cock and hen survive from one breeding season to the next they typically return together. It therefore seems as though the hens choose which male they will breed with and then remain with him for a fairly prolonged period, far longer than is necessary for pure mating – not quite the sexual free-for-all envisaged by Edward Grey.

WHY DO PHEASANTS BREED THE WAY THEY DO?

Understanding how the birds set up their territories is one thing, but it tells us little about why they do it in this particular way. It is obvious males compete and that they display to the hens – these are common features of almost all bird species. But what is it about pheasants that makes them breed in this peculiar way, one cock attracting a group of hens to his territory for a

MALE – FEMALE DISPLAYS

Ritual approach

Male walking towards female with fluffed-up body feathers, erect wattle and ear-tufts

Hen walking

Lateral display

Male's wing drooping and tail fanned to make body look as large as possible

Hen standing

Tid-bitting

Male pointing at ground with bill

Hen squatting

protracted period? To understand this we need to look more closely at what the two sexes do once they have settled on their territories.

I once spent a couple of days doing nothing from dawn to dusk but sitting in a car and watching a particular piece of woodland edge to see what the pheasants got up to on their territories – not the most exciting way to spend my time, but very informative. Starting a little before dawn, the cocks started to cackle from their roost sites and often flew down to the edge of the crop as first light was just beginning to show. This was followed by a minute or two of stretching, feeding and preening, mixed with the first crows of the day. The cocks strutted around at the edge of the cover, eyeing up the opposition on neighbouring territories and waiting for the hens. About 10–20 minutes after true dawn the hens emerged. They usually walked out of the cover and slowly moved out towards the male, feeding as they went. The cock did not seem particularly excited as the hens came out to join him, spending most of his time standing alert, keeping an eye out for any disturbance. Eventually the hens joined him and the group moved out into the growing crop. They were out for about two hours, gradually moving further and further away from the cover and spreading out from the male as they went; the hens seemed to stay closest to him when near the edge of the cover. All the time, however, the hens did little else but feed, walking slowly through the crop and picking off certain parts of the plants. Whatever they were feeding on they appeared to be very fussy. They took a few seconds between each peck, so they were not just going for volume or grazing like cattle. All the time the male stood alert, following rather than leading the hens as they searched for food. The only thing that excited the male was when another male approached too close Then he would run or fly towards the intruder and a noisy chase ensued. When this happened the hens would crouch. If the intruder found them they would try and make it back to the cover before they were forced to copulate, the usual fate of a hen caught out in the open by a strange male. After two hours or so, the hens gradually made their way back towards the cover, more closely followed by the male as they came near too, and eventually disappeared into, the undergrowth. The male now took the chance to feed himself

The size of a male's wattles are a good indicator of how territorial he is at that moment.

properly, while lazily keeping an eye out for other cocks or the chance to mate forcibly with an unwary hen.

Observing the cock and the hens when they are out feeding together is simple enough, but it leaves a number of important questions unanswered. Do the hens all live together as a group when they are in the cover? Do they nest in the male's territory? To answer these questions simple observations are not enough, it is necessary to look at information from hens fitted with radio transmitters.

In 1990, we set about collecting detailed information on the movements of both cocks and hens during the breeding season on the Wimborne St Giles estate in Dorset. We fitted radio transmitters to 50 hens and numbered neck collars to 30 cocks in February. We then followed both sexes through April to see how they all got on together. We tracked the hens three times a day to get an idea of their movements, and wrote down the positions of the cocks every time we saw them. We also recorded the size of their wattles, the erectile red tissue around their eyes. The size of the wattle seems to be a good indicator of how territorial a male is, and we mapped out the size and position of their territories only using those sightings where the wattles were fully inflated.

Pulling together all of these sightings and radiolocations showed us some interesting things. The figure shows how, in the best studied area of the estate, the birds fitted their movements together in April and where each hen finally decided to nest. First, it shows that the males spaced themselves out; none of their territories overlapped. The hen ranges, on the other hand, often overlapped with each other, which is hardly surprising as we already know that more than one female often breeds with the same male. However, the ranges of those hens that did breed with the same male were often quite distinct. Just because they chose to feed in a group with a certain male did not mean that they spent the rest of the day together. This, together with the fact that the males often remain out in the open once the hens have finished feeding, shows that they do not guard the hens when they are in cover – how could they if they all go their separate ways? Moreover, the hens' nests are usually located outside the male's

territory, and often outside the hen's own April ranges as well.

What do these observations tell us about the needs of pheasants during the breeding season? In particular, why do groups of hens decide to mate with the same male? It is worth examining the various factors that may attract a female to settle with an individual male, even if he already has other mates, and then to stay with him for such a prolonged period.

First, the male may just be providing sperm and the females may be choosing a male on the quality of his likely offspring. A big, healthy male is likely to father big, healthy chicks. This is certainly a major part of the whole exercise but, as the actual transfer of sperm only takes a few seconds, why do the females stay with the male for over a month? In other species, where it does seem that the females only want to mate, and want nothing else from the male, the mating system is based on what is known as a 'lek'. The males all stand in a group displaying, while the females come in, eye up the candidates, quickly mate and then disappear. In these species, like black grouse in Europe, or sharp-tailed grouse in North America, sperm does seem to be the female's main concern and they rarely stay with the male for longer than is necessary. So in pheasants, the male must be providing something more.

It could be that he is guarding an area of nesting cover, keeping it safe for the use of his harem. There are two problems with this idea, however. First, as we have seen, the hens usually nest outside his territory. Secondly, studies in Britain, Sweden and North America have all shown that there is no relationship between the quality of nesting cover in a male's territory and the number of hens he attracts. It is therefore extremely unlikely that access to nesting cover has anything to do with why male's set up territories or why females chose a certain male.

Another theory is that the male helps with the nest or with rearing the chicks. This is certainly the case with most bird species but for pheasants it just does not hold true. The males do not sit on the nest, they do not help rear the chicks and, even if they did, they could only help one female at a time. It would be a daft female which decided to join a male that already had a mate, as he could only help one of them.

Why does more than one hen pheasant often choose to breed with same cock?

Perhaps the male just rounds up as many females as he can and bullies them into staying so that no one else can mate with them. But this does not make sense either. The male only stays with the females when they are feeding with him in the open. For much of the day the females hide up in the cover and have little or nothing to do with him. If he were keeping them with him by force he should be guarding them all day long, as seems to happen with elk and red deer. In pheasants, there is also no sign that the male tries to keep the females with him; rather he spends his time deterring intruders. It is also the hens that initiate mating. It is quite difficult for a cock to mate with an unwilling hen and most forced attempts are unsuccessful. The females seem to be there of their own free-will and have ample opportunity to leave.

The possibilities seem to be running out. All we know for certain so far is that the male certainly provides sperm, which is hardly a surprising conclusion. Maybe it is time to take another look at what the birds actually do when they are sharing the territory. In particular, what else could the male be providing for the females?

One thing to consider is food; the main activity of the cock seems to be to stand guard while the hens are out feeding in the open. During spring, their main foods are the growing shoots of crops, together with any insects, wild seeds or waste grain they can find. This is a fairly bulky diet, particularly the growing shoots, and one fairly low in energy and protein. The hens are desperately trying to lay down fat to see them through the nesting season and they want to feed as efficiently as possible. On a diet like this, the amount of energy they can take in is limited by the rate at which it can be digested. Once they have filled their crops with enough food to keep their guts busy for the day there is no point in eating any more. In spring their guts are working as fast as possible, and they are already eating to their limit. If they cannot increase the quantity that goes in, therefore, the only two other options are to increase its quality and to avoid wasting energy

51

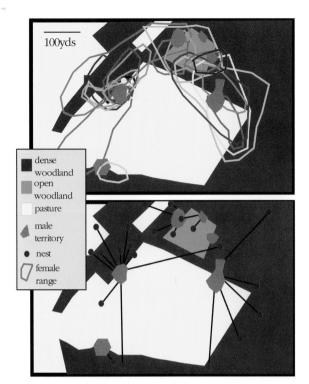

dense woodland
open woodland
pasture
male territory
nest
female range

(Top left) Intensive mapping of cock displays and the movements of radiotracked hens lets us build up a picture of how the sexes interact in the spring. The male territories are clearly separate, while the females have home ranges that overlap each other and which often cover more than one male territory.

(Bottom left) Radiotracking also lets us see how the position of the hen's nest relates to the cock's territory. The hens typically nest outside the male's territory and may even nest within the territory of a neighbouring male.

Female pheasants appear to join males of their own free will. They are not forced to stay on his territory.

Hen pheasants appear to be very selective feeders in the spring.

so that more can be saved as fat. Increasing food quality is a question of picking off the nutritious growing tips of the crop, which is why the hens are so fussy when they are out feeding. They want to make sure that they are not filling their crops with bulky, low-quality leaves, just the juiciest bits from the tips. These give them the most energy in the most concentrated form.

The idea of saving energy to increase fat is not as strange as it may sound. It has been calculated that, for birds like pheasants, running uses four times as much energy as walking, while flying is 20 times as expensive in energy terms. Given these sorts of figures it makes sense for a hen to run and fly as little as possible if she is to save energy for the nesting season. Just watching the hens during April confirms this. They seem to do everything slowly, walking lazily out of cover in the morning, carefully choosing their food and then sauntering back when they have finished. They do not even bother to look out for approaching danger, leaving that to the vigilant cock. This energy-saving policy is best described

by comparing the amount of time hens in the open spend doing different things. When the male is there they spend about 80 per cent of their time feeding, 3 per cent looking around and 12 per cent walking. If the male is not there this changes to 30 per cent feeding, 35 per cent alert and 25 per cent walking. In contrast, a territorial male spends 60 per cent of his time alert, 25 per cent feeding and 10 per cent walking when he is looking after his harem. On a territory the male acts as look-out while the hens feed; when he has gone the hen's feeding rate drops off dramatically.

What does all this tell us about the function of the territory, or what the cock might be providing for the hens? First, the hens seem interested in only three things: feeding on specific morsels of food while out in the open, returning to cover to digest their meals, and avoiding disturbance, typically from an intruding male but also from predators. The male's role seems to be to defend the females when they are out feeding. He does this by not feeding himself. He stands alert while the hens forage around his feet, especially when they are at the immediate edge of the cover, and tries to intimidate his neighbours, chasing them if they get too close. It seems as if the main thing the male is providing is protection from disturbance. This allows the females to feed in a vulnerable, open environment without having to risk being harassed by other males, eaten by a predator, or chased. Once they return to the cover they seem able to look after themselves and the cock does not have much to do with them.

If the main function of a male's territory is to give the hens undisturbed access to food, this also explains why more than one hen chooses to stay with the same male. In spring there is no shortage of food, and huge areas of growing crop become available at the same time. However, although there may be a lot of it, the quality of the food is low. The hens must be careful not to waste energy if they are to build up fat for nesting. Protection from disturbance is something that a cock can provide to more than one hen at the same time. In the same way, being in a harem may also actually make life safer for a hen. While some birds may use territories to defend a resource that is strictly limited, like suitable nest sites or food supplies, pheasants are defending something more intangible, security from disturbance. This can be given in equal quantity to many hens at the same time.

WHAT IS IT THAT MAKES CERTAIN MALES SO ATTRACTIVE?

Understanding what the male provides is one thing. What it does not explain is why some males attract more hens than others. Whatever it is that the hens are looking for in a cock, many of them seem to find it in the same one. I have seen a male with 25 hens in his harem, and ones with over a dozen are not uncommon. Three or four is more typical, but quite a few cocks fail to attract any at all, even if they manage to set up a territory. Even 25 hens should not cause any problems in terms of fertility. In North America, where they were worried about overshooting of their males, they set out to see how many hens a cock could cover before his fertility started to decline. The scientists gave up at 50, although the cocks were still going strong. There is no doubt that a cock pheasant can successfully mate with large numbers of hens. The question is why hens

Although breeding females do seem to spend most of their time with one male, are they really faithful?

in a given area often reach the same conclusion as to who they should settle with.

First, however, we should consider whether the hens really do settle with just one male. A brief look at a pheasant territory could easily lead one to the conclusion that all was peaceful. The cock stands alert while the hens feed quietly around his feet. At first sight it seems a very structured arrangement, but things are not always what they seem. Neither sex is entirely faithful and, when given the chance, they will seek to mate with outsiders.

In the case of the males this tendency is fairly obvious. They will mate with the hens of neighbouring males if the opportunity arises, which is not infrequently in a dense population. A territorial cock will place himself between his hens and an intruding male to try and prevent this, giving threat displays and, if necessary, chasing the interloper away, and this works well if there is only one intruder. But successful forced matings are most common when more than one male is involved, one distracting the territory-holder, the other sneaking in when he is busy elsewhere. I am not suggesting that gangs of males try to outwit territory-holders in a concerted attack, rather that if a male sees a group of unattended hens, he will do his best to take advantage.

Forced mating is an appropriate description for these encounters. They are violent and the female obviously wants no part in the proceedings. However, the hens will also voluntarily seek the attentions of more than one male during the mating season. The extent of this behaviour is not easy to quantify, as most of the hens look similar and, on any given morning they seem to want to stay with just one male. It is who they go with on different mornings that is interesting. Over the years we have caught hens in February and fitted them with numbered neck collars, enabling us recognise to them at a distance through binoculars. Once we can identify individual hens, it is an easy matter to see just how faithful they are by noting which males we see them with on different mornings throughout April. We can then end up with a fairly good picture of who is doing what.

The first thing to note is that the hens *do* seem to pick one male and spend the vast majority of their time on his territory. Despite this obvious bonding, however, they also pop up with different males every now and then. It appears as though the average hen spends 90 per cent of her time in her favourite male's harem and the remaining 10 per cent with other cocks. In most cases this just involves one other male, but we have seen hens appear in four different harems during April. This behaviour also seems most common in high-density populations. On my first study area on Lyons Estate in Ireland, a low-density population, I only saw one hen that changed males over three years. In contrast, in 1986, our study area on Knoll Farm in Hampshire had an exceptionally dense breeding population and 40 per cent of all our sightings of tagged hens were with males other than their usual partners.

For pheasants, mating with someone other than their usual partner makes a lot of sense. For the cocks it gives them extra chances to father chicks. For the hens it may provide insurance against their favourite male having low fertility or producing weak offspring. As most pheasants only live long enough to breed once, they want to spread the risk.

But despite their occasional straying, there does seem to be a bond between the cock and the hens in his harem. Certainly most hens spend the majority of their time with only one male. We have seen how the function of the cock's territory is to provide a secure feeding ground for the hens while they feed in the open and then retire to cover to digest their meal. While the male provides protection, the hens allow him to mate. So what can certain males provide better than others, that enables them to attract such a disproportionate number of females? One possibility is that, by establishing a particularly attractive territory, a male may be able to monopolise access to something the hens need – either dense cover or a particularly rich food source. While the hens want security from disturbance, they also want access to nutritious food and dense cover, and some cocks may hold territories that contain both in abundance.

During the springs of 1987 and 1988 we counted the number of birds breeding along over 60 miles of different sorts of woodland edge, bordering a whole range of different crop types. We found little diffference in harem size between edges rich in shrubs and those with little cover, or between those bordering cereal fields and grassland. For shrubby edges next to cereal fields,

By individually marking birds with numbered neck collars we have been able to determine how faithful they actually are. (Maureen Woodburn)

a combination rich in both cover and food, the average number of hens per cock (including territorial males that failed to attract any hens) was 1.35. For bare woodland edges next to grassland, territories that should have been short of both food and cover, the figure was 1.33. There seemed to be very little difference in the attractiveness of males in terms of either the food or cover available within their territories.

What did come out clearly from this comparison, however, was the number of territories along the different sorts of edge. We found over eight times as many territories along an edge rich in shrubby cover bordering cereals as we did along the same length of bare woodland bordering grassland. So although the individual territories were just as attractive to the hens, there

were a lot more territories in the areas rich in both food and cover. Pheasants certainly want areas rich in cover and with nutritious food, but the cocks seem to adjust their territories in response to these resources. Rather than a male monopolising a lot of shrubby cover and good food so that he can attract lots of females, it seems that good resources simply attract more territories.

One year I saw an extreme example of this on the farm where I used to live. When they were cleaning out a derelict grain store they created a huge pile of rotting corn in one corner of a farmyard, which was alive with bugs and half-fermented grain — the ideal diet for pheasants in the spring. Rather than one male monopolising this as part of his territory and attracting a huge number of hens to his harem, however, it ended up with seven or eight cocks all holding minuscule territories on different parts of the pile, each attracting a typical number of females. Improving food quality did not lead to one male gaining a super-territory; it just attracted more males.

If the hens are not choosing a male on the quality of his territory, then, what else could they be looking for? The obvious thing is the quality of the male himself. If male quality is the important thing then can we find particular features that are characteristic of the most attractive males? One thing that came very clearly out of Matt Ridley's work was that old cocks were much better at setting up territories than young ones, and then attracted eight times as many hens to their harems. The age and experience of the cock is therefore very important, but there is much more to it than that. Even amongst birds of the same age, some are particularly attractive.

In Sweden there has been a lot of work measuring the physical features of different males during the winter and then seeing which ones get the most hens in the spring. They find that the most obvious feature of a successful male is that he has long spurs, and I am sure that this is true. Older males do have longer spurs and, as weapons, they are important when it comes to the males deciding which is dominant.

But I have some doubts about whether the hens actually go out and choose which male they are going to breed with simply on the length of his spurs. First, it is very hard to see a male's spurs from any distance. One year we tried fitting our birds with leg rings to mark them and it was virtually impossible to see them properly unless they were standing on a road. Even short grass can hide the lower part of the leg from sight. Moreover, the display that males give to females when they are trying to attract them into their harem, the 'lateral display', completely hides the spurs from the hen. If they were so important, I am sure the cocks would try to show them to the hens, not hide them away behind their wings. I think that long spurs help a male make himself dominant and old males usually have long spurs. But I doubt that they are of particular importance from the hen's viewpoint when

The quality of the food and cover along a woodland edge seems to determine how many territories that area will hold, but does not influence the success of the males that chose those territories.

she decides who to settle and mate with.

Part of the problem with the Swedish work is that their study birds are kept in pens all winter, the period when the cocks are establishing dominance. They are then released for study in the spring. If the hens spend all winter watching the cocks fighting, and the long-spurred males winning, then it is hardly surprising that they find these same males attractive when they are released in the spring. Certainly, our own studies of birds that have been free-living all winter have found no evidence that the hens prefer long-spurred mates when it comes to the breeding season, apart from the fact that they like old cocks.

Nigella Hillgarth, another Oxford student, looked at penned pheasants to see what it was that the hens were looking for in a male. She let hens into small pens where they had a choice of four males which were all strangers to them, each held in neighbouring pens. She found that the hens went for the males which had the largest and reddest wattles, the inflatable patches of skin around their eyes. She also found that cocks with certain parasitic infections tended to have pale wattles and were not as attractive to the hens. We have also seen the same thing in the field. The males with the biggest, most colourful wattles tend to end up with more hens, and dosing cocks to get rid of parasitic worms in the spring can lead to larger, redder wattles and make them much more attractive to the hens.

The trouble with all of this is that it is virtually impossible to separate out what is most important to the hens. A big, healthy male may well have long spurs, large wattles, glossy plumage and a long tail. He may also be one that displays well, crows loudly, can defeat intruding males and is resistant to disease. I am sure that the hens assess a whole range of different male characteristics before they settle to mate, just as humans do. What seems clear is that they look for fit, healthy-looking males, ones that can protect them while they are out feeding and which stand a better chance of fathering similarly fit, healthy chicks. I am sure that the hen's decision on who to mate with is based on the male's characteristics rather than the quality of his territory, but I doubt whether there is a single answer as to what features they find attractive. Maybe they just fall in love!

WHAT DETERMINES THE NUMBER OF TERRITORIES IN AN AREA?

Understanding the function of pheasant territories is one thing, but using this knowledge to help management is quite another. All this work on territories may seem rather academic, but it can give us clear pointers for management. Understanding the birds' requirements is the essential first step to knowing what we can do to help them. One integral part of managing pheasants is understanding how many breeding birds a piece of land can hold and this is obviously linked to the potential number of territories.

One of the hardest things about being a game biologist is explaining what one does for a living. The response is often 'Oh, you work on pheasants, you must be a gamekeeper', or more irritatingly 'Are you a pheasant plucker?' When I try to describe my job it often boils down to counting pheasants. 'Why, I can do that', comes the reply. 'one two three four . . .' But counting pheasants is an integral part of the job and provides the basic information that we need to try and make sense of their lives. One of the easiest things to count is the number of crowing males in an area. This is something the Americans have relied on heavily as it allows them to monitor populations quickly and cheaply over large areas. All sorts of things will set cock pheasants crowing in the spring – another crowing cock, a slammed door or a back-firing car. The Americans have even used small charges of explosives thrown into fields to help them get good counts of the number of cocks nearby – a technique I wanted to try when I was working in Ireland, but was advised against. The birds also seem to be particularly sensitive to earth tremors. They crow wildly a few moments before earthquakes hit. This makes them particularly popular with residents in vulnerable areas – enough for them to be the national bird of a number of countries.

The trouble with just counting the crowing males is that it gives one very little information on the hens. Although an area that contains a lot of calling males almost certainly also holds a lot of females, it is not good enough for really detailed monitoring of year-to-year changes in their numbers. The reason for this is that there only appear to be a limited number of suitable sites for territories in any one area. The birds are

Cock pheasants will start crowing in response to all sorts of stimuli: earthquakes, explosions or slammed car doors. (Alexis de la Serre)

quite specific in what they need for a territory and different males use the same plots year after year. I once spent a morning talking to a farmer's wife who insisted that the same male had held a territory in her garden for the last ten years, even though he seemed to be a different colour each time!

Knoll Farm, one of our long-term monitoring sites, has held around 30 territorial males every year since the early 1980s when we started counting. In these same years the number of females has varied from 150 to 40. The non-territorial males have numbered between 20 and 70. Obviously, if the total number of males on the area fell below 30 then some of the territories would have to stay empty. But this is rarely the case in Britain, where birds surviving from previous releases usually ensure that there are more males than suitable territories. This can cause problems with cock-crow counts. If all the territories are full, they cannot really measure population changes. This approach only works if there are more territories than males.

Of course, the number of territories in an area can change. After the strong winds of the late 1980s, Clarendon Park, another of our main study areas, lost a great many of its trees, particularly along the edges of some of the roads running through a 1,000 acre wood in the centre of the estate. Before these winds, the middle of this big wood was too dark and dense for birds to set up territories. Afterwards, the open areas attracted quite reasonable numbers of new territorial males.

Because of this, we try to count both the number of territorial males and their females each spring. This is my favourite job of the year. Starting just after dawn, the idea is to drive around an area, usually a 250 acre block of land, and to scan every hedgerow, woodland edge or block of standing cover through binoculars. Just seeing birds is no use, we have to be fairly sure that we have recorded *every* bird on the area. It has to be done from a car as the birds are usually quite unperturbed unless we get out. On a good morning, most of the birds are out on their territories, the males standing guard while the females feed nearby. We start in mid-March, and although at this time many of the hens are still in their winter flocks, by early April the hens have usually settled down with their chosen males and it is fairly easy to get a consistent count. Just to be sure, we count each area three times on different days and combine the counts, trying to see which birds were missed on any one count, to get a total. We have even checked the accuracy by counting areas where most of the birds carry numbered tags around their necks, so that we know exactly which bird we see each time.

On an area well supplied with tracks and fairly flat ground, this can be pretty straightforward, especially if you know your way around. The problems come when you turn up at a new area, perhaps even without a decent map, and try to find your way around every rut-riddled track at dawn. Four-wheel drive and a winch are essential, but I have lost count of the number of times I have been stuck. One of the most embarrassing occasions was when I got lost on a track where it was impossible to reverse or turn back. I ended up on the neatly manicured lawn of the neighbouring farmer's back garden. When I did counts in Utah it was just as bad, as many of the farmers would never agree to have a Wildlife Department

We count the numbers of breeding pheasants in April by scanning an area from a car. (Roger Draycott)

truck on their land. It was a question of sneaking in and out before they got up. I was only caught three times that year.

Knowing what the birds are looking for in the spring is one thing, but understanding how this influences the number of birds that will settle to breed in an area is quite another. Our counts aim to do more than just discover what the birds want in terms of a territory. Over the last ten years we have been doing counts all over Britain, as well as in parts of North America, Ireland, Austria and China. The idea has been to try and see what it is that makes some areas particularly good at holding high breeding densities, and whether the birds are looking for the same things the world over – there is not much point coming up with a perfect description of good pheasant breeding habitat for one area if it does not work elsewhere as well.

At present we have counts from just over 100,000 acres of ground, scattered all over the world, some from single 250 acre blocks counted in just one year, others from the same sites counted every year since 1982. All in all it gives us a broad-ranging set of data to work with. In each area we count the number of territories, the number of hens with each male and the number of non-territorial males. We then map out the main habitat types in each area, both the crops and the types of woodland, scrub, reed, rough grass or other habitats that might be of use to the birds. The figure opposite gives a range of the different sorts of maps we collect, with examples of both the best and worst. Bear in mind that these are just a handful of examples; our findings are actually based on far more detailed habitat descriptions and many more maps than can easily be presented here.

I have split the habitats into two very broad types: agricultural crops, which are presented in white, and different types of standing cover, which are coloured. The first thing that is clear is that pheasants reach their highest breeding densities where there is a good mixture of the two. The Grantsville example from Utah shows what happens when agricultural crops predominate. Although there was a good range of crop types, the only cover was a single strip of uncut grass along one roadside. As a consequence, no pheasants settled to breed in the square, although some were present on the neighbouring land. The Clarendon Park example shows the effect of too much cover. A large block of commercial forestry, although quite good cover in itself, covers almost the whole of the square; the few birds breeding in the area are clustered around the edges of the fields. Clarendon Park itself contains some excellent breeding areas, but not in this part. The Benson example, also from Utah, shows some improvement. Here the crops and cover are starting to be more mixed. Scrubby woodland and reeds along the edges of the Bear River border on agricultural land and breeding densities are noticeably higher than in the previous examples. It is also worth considering where the birds are setting up their territories; in each case

Examples of breeding pheasant counts from different areas. Each map relates to a square kilometre (250 acre) count. Agricultural fields are given in white, CER=cereal, GR=grass, PLO=plough, STUB=stubble, MAIZE=sweet corn, ALF=alfalfa (lucerne), RGR=rough grass.

they are where cover borders on open ground. The length of boundary between cover and crop seems to be an important factor influencing how many birds decide to breed in an area. Knoll Farm shows this same effect; the territories clustered along the woodland edges and, as this site had a good mixture of cover and crop, the breeding density was higher still. Knoll Farm also shows another point of interest: the birds seem to set up more territories along shrubby woodland edges than on bare edges. Seefeld in Austria shows the same effect, with territories clustered along the reed and shrubby edges, with lower numbers along the other borders. This square in Seefeld is also one of the highest breeding densities I have ever come across: a good mixture of cover and crop and lots of edge, leading to 46 breeding hens per 100 acres. It is still a lot less than the record of 88 hens per 100 acres on Pelee Island, a site I shall say more about later, but still very respectable.

All of these examples come from areas within the pheasant's introduced range. How do they compare with native populations in China? Zhang Zheng-wang carried out pheasant counts in three different parts of China and found an average of 2.5 territories per 100 acres. These are similar to the densities I found in Utah, but in Britain our counts average two to three times higher. Although there is a huge variation in the density of territories in different areas, China seems to

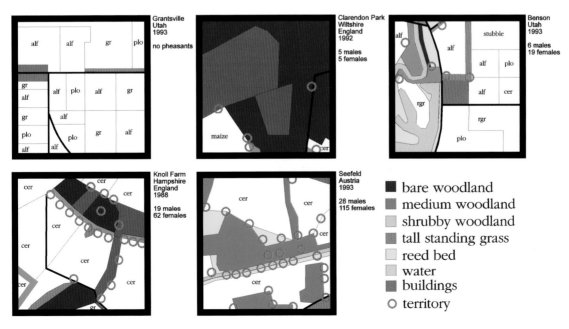

Grantsville
Utah
1993

no pheasants

Clarendon Park
Wiltshire
England
1992

5 males
5 females

Benson
Utah
1993

6 males
19 females

Knoll Farm
Hampshire
England
1988

19 males
62 females

Seefeld
Austria
1993

28 males
115 females

■ bare woodland
■ medium woodland
□ shrubby woodland
■ tall standing grass
□ reed bed
□ water
■ buildings
○ territory

hold rather lower, but generally similar, numbers to many parts of their introduced range.

By considering all the different areas we have counted, it is possible to draw some broad conclusions about how the amount of different types of cover affects the number of breeding birds. As the few examples here show, the quality and quantity of cover and edges are the main factors. Overall, our counts show that there is one territory per 300 yards of edge. The more edge, the more birds will settle to breed. The length of edge in an area is closely related to the amount of cover there is. If there is little cover, there will obviously not be much edge. As the amount of cover increases, so too does the amount of edge, but only up to a certain point. Once there is too much cover, the blocks start to join together and the amount of edge decreases, the cut-off point seems to be when around 30-40 per cent of an area is cover as opposed to crop.

The examples above show this clearly. Grantsville had virtually no cover, no edge and no pheasants. Benson was better, with about 10 per cent cover and 1,500 yards of edge bordering onto cropland, holding six territories. Knoll Farm was better again: 20 per cent cover, 3,500 yards of edge and 19 territories. Seefeld came in at close to the optimum, with around 30-40 per cent cover, 6,000 yards of edge and a high number of territories. The Clarendon square then shows what happens with too much cover, about 90 per cent in this case: only 1,000 yards of edge and the number of territories has fallen to only five.

After this, the quality of the edge comes into play. Along woodland edges, the amount of shrubby cover seems to be the main point of interest. On really shrubby edges, the average rises to one territory per 150–200 yards; on bare, draughty ones that provide little cover for the birds it can go down to one territory per 500 yards or even less. Having a lot of edge is one thing, but it must be of the right sort if it is to hold any appreciable number of birds. The pheasants' preference for the edges of dense cover in the spring is seen again and again. In China, Zhang Zheng-wang found that the cover selected for use as territories by his birds contained 20 times more cover between 1 and 2 metres in height than was typical in the area. In Britain we find that dense cover at the same height is heavily selected by territorial birds. The same holds true in Utah and in John Carroll's studies in Pennsylvania.

The quantity and quality of edges between cover and agricultural crops are the main factors influencing how many birds, of both sexes, decide to breed in an area. An intimate mix of crops and cover leads to a good quantity of edge. Careful management of the cover can increase its quality, in particular the shrubby cover it provides. What then about the types of agricultural crops? How do these affect breeding densities?

When the birds are looking for somewhere to settle in the spring, the crop types can be important in a number of different ways. They could be looking for crops that provide good nesting cover, the quality of the food could be important, or the height of the crop may affect their visibility and protection from predators. It is worth looking at each of these in turn.

First, do the birds set up territories next to certain crops because they provide a good nesting habitat? If this was the case we would expect to find more territories on edges bordering winter cereals than spring ones, next to alfalfa rather than maize, and most of all where cover borders on tall, rough grass still standing from the previous year. Yet birds set up the same number of territories if the crop is either a winter or spring cereal, even though winter cereals provide better nesting cover. They do not seem to mind if the crop is alfalfa or newly sown maize, even though alfalfa is a very popular nesting site and maize is one of the worst. If anything they set up fewer territories where the crop is rough grass, a very attractive habitat for nesting compared to other crop types. This suggests that the quality of nesting cover has little to do with the position of the territories and is not what the birds are looking for in the crop.

If the birds are looking for crops that provide concealment from predators then why are the territories set up along the edges of cover? A typical territory has a mixture of open feeding areas and dense cover, so cover is important, but the birds also need open areas. It may be that the cocks seek out places where they can be seen displaying. I think there may be some truth in this, but it is not the whole answer. If this were all there is to it, why do the hens spend so long out in the open with them, far longer than is necessary just to eye them up and be mated?

The main interest in open ground, therefore, seems to be the quality of food it can provide. We looked at our data on breeding densities and a couple of pictures started to emerge. Pheasants seem to set up more territories along edges bordering on cultivated land – wheat, barley, maize, etc. – than next to grassland. In early spring the birds need a highly nutritious food, and agricultural land seems the best source, with a mixture of growing shoots, waste grain and seeds from the previous year. Grassland, on the other hand, tends to be short on nutrition and has little in the way of waste seeds in most areas. As a result it is not surprising that we find over three times the number of both cocks and hens along the edges of arable ground that we do grassland.

The best example I can think of to demonstrate the importance of food quality on the number of birds that settle to breed in an area came from an experiment we did on Clarendon Park. With the changes that have occurred in modern agriculture in Britain in recent years we were concerned that the birds were short of food in the spring. In particular, the loss of stubble fields and more efficient harvesting meant that there was little in the way of seeds for the birds. Although there was no shortage of growing shoots from different crops, it still seemed that the hens were not getting an adequate diet to build up body condition for the nesting period. We decided to resolve this by placing two feed hoppers full of

grain in each cock territory to supplement the birds' diet. The birds certainly liked them and ended up taking over half their diet from these sources. More interestingly, where we had once had one territory, we now found that we often had two, one cock guarding each hopper. By supplementing the natural food availability we had been able to raise the attractiveness of the area to both sexes and increase overall breeding density. There was nothing more telling than to look along a woodland edge early in the morning and see a cock standing just out from each of the hoppers while the hens were busy filling their crops with grain. The whole point of the pheasant's breeding system is that the cocks provide the hens with safe access to nutritious food. By laying out hoppers in such a way that each cock could defend one we used this knowledge to give the birds just what they needed in a form they could defend and feed from in safety. They in turn responded and more birds chose to breed in the area, a simple and effective management result.

From a management viewpoint this work gives a number of very clear pointers. When the birds disperse from their winter covers they move directly to their territories. The number of birds

The number of cock territories in an area is closely linked to the quality of the habitat. (Alexis de la Serre)

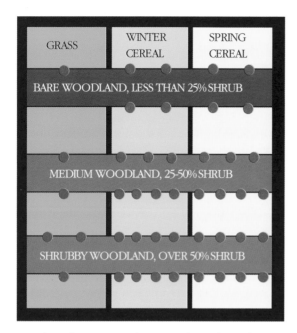

GRASS	WINTER CEREAL	SPRING CEREAL
BARE WOODLAND, LESS THAN 25% SHRUB		
MEDIUM WOODLAND, 25-50% SHRUB		
SHRUBBY WOODLAND, OVER 50% SHRUB		

Our breeding counts let us work out how the cover along different woodland edges interacts with the crop type in the neighbouring field to influence the density of male territories. This illustration shows how the number of cock territories per kilometre (red circles) varies along different combinations of woodland edge and crop type.

that choose to settle in an area is closely linked to the number of suitable territories. These are areas where dense cover borders on open ground. Although the sorts of cover and the crops on which the birds feed vary around the world, the principle remains the same. To increase the number of birds that settle in an area it seems sensible to try and increase the number of territories. There are three ways of doing this: first by increasing the length of edge between cover and open ground; secondly by raising the quality of the cover to increase its attractiveness to the birds; and lastly by increasing the quality of their food. This can be done by either planting nutritious crops such as cereals or by placing small hoppers along the edges of the cover where they can easily be defended by the males.

Territories are much more than simply crowing or display areas for the males. They are a vital part of the requirements of both sexes. Understanding what the birds need from these areas helps us design management options to increase their numbers. But there is more to management than simply increasing the number of breeding birds – these birds must also breed effectively.

By placing small feeding hoppers along woodland edges we were able to increase the number of territories that were established.

NESTS

After following the birds through the first part of the breeding season, when the cocks and hens are very visible and spend much of their time out on their territories, it comes as a shock when the hens start to disappear to nest. For biologists this means a sudden shift in workload. After being able simply to go out in the morning and see the birds doing their thing in the open, suddenly they find that they do all in their power to avoid being seen, and spend their time hidden away in the most inaccessible places they can find. Studying nesting pheasants is a real problem and the most interesting part of their year is the most difficult to study. Despite, or perhaps because of, this, a huge amount of effort has gone into finding out what they do and where, how well they do it and what goes wrong.

A huge amount of research has been devoted to the nesting success and habits of the hen pheasant.

LAYING

Hen pheasants will normally start to breed in the year after their birth. These young hens are usually lighter than older birds, but still start laying just as well and produce quality eggs. However, I once came across a hen that laid a single egg in her first September. She was being kept in a pen as breeding stock for the next year and was no more then four months old when she produced. The egg was only about half normal size so it would not have been much good even if it had arrived at the appropriate time.

In Britain, hens usually start laying eggs in the middle of April while they are still spending much of their time with the male on his territory. They usually leave the territory to nest in the most attractive nearby cover, and the nest itself is no more than a scrape on the ground. It takes time to fill a nest with eggs, and during the laying period hens only visit the nest once or sometimes twice a day, leaving the eggs uncovered when they are away with the male. Once the clutch is complete they then begin incubation and will sit on the eggs almost continuously until they hatch.

The average pheasant nest contains about 11 eggs but there is considerable variation; nests laid early in the breeding season average 14 or 15 eggs, while this drops to only 8 or 9 for renests later in the summer. The biggest nest I have seen had 21 eggs, produced by one of the first hens I ever radiotracked. Roy Perks, the gamekeeper at Clarendon Park, used to spend a lot of time collecting pheasant eggs from the estate to rear in his incubators. He once found a nest with 54 eggs in it which must be close to a record. Nests as large as this are certainly the work of more than one hen, something I will return to later. At the opposite extreme I have also heard of hens sitting on a single egg, although the smallest incubated clutch I have actually seen contained four.

The ability of the hen to lay more than one clutch is also well known. If their first nest is lost, most hens will go on to produce a second, sometimes a third and rarely a fourth. Of about 600 hen pheasants that we have followed with radio-telemetry, however, only one has produced four nests, all of which were lost so that she never actually hatched a chick. Renesting is most common when the hen loses her nest during laying. If this happens she will often just choose another site and continue producing eggs with no delay. If she has already started to incubate them when they are lost it will often take her a few days to get back into the rhythm of producing more eggs and she may be less likely to bother. The longer she has been incubating, the longer it will take her to start egg production again. A rarer occurrence is for a hen to produce another nest after successfully hatching a brood of chicks and then losing them in their first few days of life. There was considerable debate about whether or not this could happen until people started radio-tracking birds. Now we know it happens, but it is not particularly common.

For most of the world it seems to be true that a hen will only successfully rear one brood of chicks per year. The summers are too short to rear more. However, in New Zealand the summers are long and mild. Kaj Westerskov, a Danish biologist who studied pheasants there in the 1950s, has some evidence that New Zealand hens can, very occasionally, rear two broods a year. His evidence is not absolutely certain but, given the length of the summers, it is just possible. There are also rumours of the same thing happening in southern China, although I have not seen any conclusive evidence.

The only other case I have come across was at Clarendon Park. Andrew Hoodless and Roger Draycott were radiotracking hens as part of the feeding experiment mentioned in the last chapter. One of their hens had just hatched a clutch and was seen every day feeding with them on a pile of farmyard muck at the back of a cattle shed. Hens usually look after the chicks on their own, with no help from the male, but in this case there was often a cock close by. It was an odd situation, but not entirely unexpected given that muck heaps are good feeding sites for both sexes. What really surprised Roger was that one day, when the chicks were about ten days old, he arrived to check the brood and could see no sign of the hen. The chicks were still there, feeding around the cock, and so he homed in on the hen's radio signal to find out what had happened to her. It turned out that she was sitting on a clutch of four eggs about 30 yards away from her brood. Over the next few days they tried to keep a close eye on these particular birds and it emerged that the hen was in the middle of laying a new clutch of

Pheasant nests regularly contain anything between 5 and 15 eggs.

eggs. Most mornings she would leave the brood in the care of the male and go off to drop another egg in the nest.

As far as I know this account is unique in two ways. First, it is the only time I have heard of a cock actively helping to rear the chicks. Secondly, I think it is the only record of a hen laying a second nest when she still had chicks alive from a previous brood. I must admit that when they first told me what they had seen I was pretty dubious. Andrew and I drove up to look and, sure enough, there was the cock, the hen and at least one chick, feeding together. As we sat and watched, the hen appeared and squatted in front of the male, the classic invitation to mate, and the male obliged. Although the hen seemed to be trying to produce two successful broods, however, it did not work out. Although the cock was seen with the brood whenever the hen was absent, the brood gradually dwindled away. After about ten days the last chick was lost and the hen's second nest was taken by a badger, so it all came to nothing.

Producing eggs is an expensive business for the hens, a considerable drain on their energy resources. Hen pheasants also appear to do everything they can to lay a good clutch of eggs, regardless of the long-term effects this may have on their survival. A well-fed hen will lay down reserves of fat during the early spring which it will then use to fuel its developing reproductive organs and the eggs they produce. The interesting thing is that a poorly fed hen in the wild will go through the same process and still produce a similar number of eggs of the same quality as its well-fed counterpart. The difference is that, after laying a clutch of eggs, the poorly fed bird may have burned up so much of its fat that it has little left to see it through the rigours of incubation and looking after the chicks. In experiments with penned birds, where the eggs are removed every day to keep the hens laying, the only difference is that poorly fed birds stop laying sooner. However, this is an artificial situation; in the wild even underfed hens seem to be able to lay enough eggs to complete a normal clutch. As a consequence, all the studies of pheasant clutch size from around the world show very similar results in terms of eggs laid in each nest, the hatchability of the eggs and their weight. What does differ is the amount of energy the hen has left to see her through the rest of the breeding season.

Hen pheasants must feed intensively to build up body condition to see them through the rigours of nesting.

A good illustration of this comes from the feeding experiment we carried out at Clarendon Park in 1994. We were worried that the reared hens in this area were losing too much fat during the laying period. To try and resolve this we placed feed hoppers full of wheat in each cock's territory in some areas and left the birds in other areas unfed. In February, when we started this system, the hens in both areas were carrying about 70 grams of body fat. By the end of April, the hens in the fed areas had increased their body fat by 11 per cent, but on the unfed areas the hens had lost 60 per cent of their fat reserves. Despite this, the hens in both areas started laying eggs at the same time, produced clutches of the same size and with eggs of similar hatchability. So hen pheasants seem to sacrifice their own body condition to ensure that they lay a quality clutch of eggs. This can have important knock-on effects. The hens on the unfed areas went on to suffer rather higher rates of mortality, and were less likely, and took longer, to initiate another clutch if they lost their first nest. As a consequence, the hens on the fed areas hatched 50 per cent more chicks than their unfed counterparts.

Of course, a hen that has burned up her fat stores to produce eggs can try to build them up again by feeding; but time spent off the nest is full of risk, and can endanger both the hen and her eggs. As a result, nesting hens try to stay on the nest as long as possible. Andrew Hoodless saw what may be the fastest feeding period by a nesting pheasant. He had been checking a group of radiotagged hens who were nesting in a clump of nettles on one of our fed areas. He was sitting in the car writing up his data when he saw one of the hens emerge from the nettles, run across the farmyard to the nearest hopper and feed non-stop for about five minutes. She then turned and ran straight back to the nettles and onto her nest. This contrasts with the experience of Rufus Sage, who followed one hen throughout her nesting period. This hen spent much of her

This radiotagged hen was in very poor condition when we recaught her after nesting. Her breast bone is clearly visible as she has lost most of the muscle from her chest.

On occasion, hen pheasants will lay eggs in the nests of other birds, in this case a woodcock's.
(David Hill)

time off the nest feeding, so much so that he often thought she had abandoned her nest. Rather than the normal 24 or 25 days of incubation, this hen spent so much time away that it took 40 days for the eggs to hatch. Even then only a few hatched successfully; most had died within the egg. And those chicks that did come off were all dead within a day.

I would love to be able to study how the amount of time a hen spends off the nest affects her chances of hatching the chicks successfully, but it is a very difficult thing to get to grips with. I recently heard of a Swedish study where an electronic thermometer hidden inside an egg was used to record how often the hen left the nest during incubation. The idea was that, every time the hen left the nest, the eggs cooled and this could give a complete picture of when, and for how long, each hen left the nest. Although I cannot prove it, I suspect that long or repeated trips away from the nest to feed are a bad thing for the eggs. Every time the hen leaves the nest she leaves a trail of scent for predators to follow. She also tramples the vegetation and can leave visual clues for predators such as crows which specialise in finding nests. Roy Perks, the Clarendon keeper, used to be a very effective egg collector to supply his rearing system. His best trick was to go out early on a morning when the grass and crops were wet with dew. He could then clearly see the tracks made by hens leaving their nests to feed and follow them back to find the eggs. If a human can key into this then I am sure that predators with sharper eyes and better noses can also use the same principle to find hens that stray too often from the nest. We will have

to wait for the results of the Swedish study to be sure.

Of course, it is also possible for a hen to be in such poor condition that she cannot even lay a proper clutch of eggs. Experiments with penned birds on very restricted diets have proved this, but it does not seem to happen much in the wild. The only case I know of was from one of our studies. The hens were surviving released birds in an area of rough grassland, very poor quality feed for the birds, which were also heavily infected with parasites: large numbers of a worm called *Heterakis* in their guts, numerous ticks on their bodies and evidence of coccidiosis, a protozoan disease of the gut. In this area the hens produced clutches about a third smaller than normal. We did not measure their fat content but it was common to see birds in a very weakened condition and those that we did manage to weigh were obviously emaciated. Of course, in a case like this it is impossible to say whether it was poor food, parasites or something else that was the cause of the problem. Suffice it to say that 95 per cent of the hens died during the breeding season and they failed to rear a chick beyond a few days of age.

EGG DUMPING

One thing that pheasants are particularly prone to doing is dropping eggs, either straight onto the ground or into the nests of other birds. They usually lay in other pheasant nests, but they can do so in almost anything. I have heard of pheasant eggs being found in a wide variety of different birds' nests: various ducks, partridge, wild turkey, grouse and woodcock. The results can be quite dramatic. The very large pheasant nests of thirty or more eggs are almost certainly the result of more than one hen, and I have also heard of a hen grey partridge found sitting on a huge pile of eggs, 16 of her own and a similar number of pheasant eggs. In North America there are also frequent accounts of the birds just leaving odd eggs lying around in the fields.

Some people have claimed that this egg dumping is the unnatural behaviour of a species taken from its true home in China and expected to live in a foreign country. This cannot be true; however, as Zhang Zheng-wang has found ring-necked pheasant eggs in the nests of silver pheasants in China and there are also records there of clutches too big to be the result of just one hen. Dumping seems to be a common feature of pheasants in both their native and their introduced ranges.

Egg dumping seems particularly common early in the season. It appears from records of nests collected by birdwatchers in Britain, that about 1–2 per cent of pheasant eggs are laid outside the hen's own nest and that about 7% of pheasant nests contain eggs from more than one female. No one really knows why they might do this or why it is particularly common early in the season. From the hen's viewpoint it might make sense to have some of her eggs in other hens' nests, in case her own is destroyed, and it is presumably easier to find other hens' nests early in the season. But if this is the explanation why do the Americans find so many single eggs just dropped, apparently at random. What I think is happening is that when the hens first come into lay their first few eggs are produced at irregular intervals; it takes time for some hens to produce an egg almost daily. For those hens whose first couple of eggs may arrive at an interval of three or four days, it makes little sense to start a nest of their own until things are in full swing. Eggs left lying around for a week or two before the others are laid could attract predators, and in any case their fertility is probably dubious. For a hen in this situation it makes more sense to get rid of these eggs somewhere else rather than putting them in her own nest. Where better than in another hen's nest? In an area where hens are thin on the ground, or where there is particularly abundant nesting cover, it may not be easy for a hen to find another pheasant nest. In these circumstances eggs appear in the nests of other species or just dropped where the hen happens to be at that time. Once the hens' reproductive system comes into regular egg production the need to get rid of these odd ones disappears and they seem to settle down to looking after them all themselves.

I often wonder what happens to the chicks that hatch from eggs dumped into other species' nests. There are certainly accounts of grey partridges whose broods include pheasant chicks and even film footage of a mixed brood in a documentary about partridges. Many partridge keepers view pheasants as a pest, as egg dumping can cause the partridge hen to abandon her nest. I have also heard of a hen mallard seen swimming with a pheasant chick perched on her back! However I doubt whether many of these fostered chicks ever survive.

There may even be more to it than this. In one of our study areas we followed a radiotagged hen which appeared to be incubating a clutch of eggs normally. To our surprise, we arrived one day to find a different hen, also fitted with a transmitter, sitting on the eggs. The original hen did not seem to mind and, a week or two later, proceeded to start another nest nearby. The hen that had taken over her first nest lost the whole clutch to a fox. John Carroll also has a similar story. Two hens were both sitting on clutches of eggs but then, halfway through incubation, they switched. In this case things turned out better for them and both successfully hatched. Why should hens do such strange things? At present there is no way of knowing but I wonder whether in these cases the hens might be sisters which have both mated with the same cock. Certainly it would make more sense in evolutionary terms if the birds involved were closely related.

HOW DO HENS DECIDE WHERE TO NEST?

There has probably been more written about where hen pheasants choose to nest than about any other part of their lives. For North America alone there are something like 100 scientific articles describing nest site selection: how this changes through the season, how successful nests are in different habitats, the humidity and light penetration into the nests and the plant species found near nests. Despite all this work however, the answer is really quite simple. Pheasants like to nest in cover that will hide them from predators while still allowing them to move on and off the nest with relative ease. They therefore tend to pick areas of rank grass or other similar cover which are not too dense overhead. The sorts of habitats that best meet their requirements change throughout the season. Early nests are started before many plants or crops have grown enough to be suitable. First nests tend to be in areas of standing vegetation left over from the previous year – long grass, weedy patches or woodland. As the summer progresses the choice widens and many later nests are found in growing crops.

This all sounds quite straightforward, so why have there been so many scientific reports

Hen pheasants will nest in a wide variety of different habitat types. (John Carroll)

looking at the fine details? There seems to be one main reason for all these studies. The success rate of pheasant nests varies a great deal between different types of nesting cover. If scientists could work out how to make a cover crop that was both attractive to the hens, and guaranteed them a high chance of success, then it ought to mean an increase in the number of birds. It seems a simple and attractive idea, but no one has ever really managed to make it work properly. This is certainly not through a lack of trying: the number of published studies says something about the amount of effort, and the funds, devoted to providing different sorts of nesting cover each year. In the early 1980s the Americans estimated they were spending over $30 million a year on planting pheasant nesting cover alone.

What happens when people try to provide nesting cover? First, it's fairly easy to come up with a recipe for a good nesting crop – there are certainly enough studies to go on. The best cover seems to be areas of tussocky grasses that are left uncut, providing some standing vegetation early in the spring. If you were to plant some of this, as often as not you would get some nesting

pheasants and they would hatch off well. The problem is that the number of birds you would get would vary incredibly. Even if they do manage to hatch a lot of chicks, you do not seem to end up with many more birds the next year. For example, during the late 1970s the Iowa Wildlife Department planted areas of dense nesting cover, a mix of alfalfa, sweet clover and wheat grass, in different counties. This proved to be good nesting cover. Some attracted high numbers of nesting birds while others hardly attracted any. Why should some areas be so much more attractive than others if they were planted up in the same way? The differences could not be explained by differences in the plots. I believe their mixed results reflect the quality of the other habitat types near each plot. If the other habitats that pheasants need are absent then even the best nesting cover in the world will not bring them into an area. Another example comes from Illinois. Here, they started a programme of planting up roadside verges with particularly good nesting cover and found that they were well

Tall grassy cover can be a preferred and successful site for nesting hens. (John Carroll)

used by the birds. The problem was that, after a few years of increases, the population crashed to a low level. The nesting sites may have been good but they obviously were not what the population really needed.

Giving the birds somewhere safe and attractive to nest seems to be common sense. Why then are the results not more positive? Obviously there are cases where it has worked, but it is certainly not guaranteed that it will. There is no doubt that providing nesting cover is a good idea. The problem is that planting nesting cover with no consideration for the hens' other requirements is a waste of time, and this is all too often what happens.

In the section on management I will discuss how nesting cover must be considered as only one of four different habitat types that are needed in an area if the birds are to reach high densities. It is as important as any other habitat type, but it is not the be-all and end-all of wild pheasant management. In particular it must be placed reasonably near to the spring territories if the birds are to make use of it, and it must be close to good feeding areas for the chicks if many of them are to survive.

In the previous chapter, I described what the birds need in terms of territories. These are more than just crowing areas for the males; they also provide an important resource for the hens, so important that the males find it useful to monopolise them to give them access to the females. How far then do the hens move from the territories to nest?

The first thing to consider is that the hens are producing eggs during the time they spend with the cock on his territory. Common sense says that they must be able to get backwards and forwards from the territory to the nest in a reasonable time and without the risk of covering uncharted ground. Consequently it is not surprising that the first nests they lay are never far from the cock's territory. We have radiotracking evidence from around 80 hens where we know which cocks they spent their time with, the extent of the males' territory and the position of their nests. The average distance moved from the centre of the territories to the nest was 200 yards. Given that a cock's terri

tory is usually only about 100 yards across, in Britain at least, this means that most hens nest near the edge of the area the cock defends.

There is certainly no tendency for the hens always to nest inside the territory; the cock is defending their feeding grounds not their eventual nest sites. Some hens will nest in this defended area, but many more choose sites on the periphery or outside it. Some even nest in the territory of the male next door. What I think is happening is that the hens choose a male to mate with on his appearance. It may be the vigour with which he displays, the size of his wattles or spurs – it is hard to be sure. One thing is fairly certain, the hens' choice does not seem to have much to do with the amount of nesting cover nearby. Hen pheasants do not seem to be over-blessed with foresight. Only once they have chosen a male and been mated do they start to think about where to nest. There is no doubt that some habitats are better than others when it comes to nesting, but the hens have already cast their die. They must make do with the best of whatever is near to their chosen cock's territory. An example of the problems this can lead to comes from Seefeld in

Hen pheasants do not choose a male on the basis of the nesting cover his territory may contain.

Austria. Although the owners do what they can to help the birds, there are times when their crop rotations lead to one part of the farm being short of suitable crops for nesting birds. In one case a ditch bordered with scrub ran across the centre of two large fields. Although the scrub was attractive enough for a number of cocks and hens to settle on territories, both fields were to be planted with maize. During April they were nothing but bare ground. A good number of hens chose to settle with the cocks in this area, despite the fact that the crops would not be any use when it came to providing them with nesting cover and the thin shrub belt was the only cover around. Hen pheasants just do not seem to think ahead and it is up to the manager to plan things in order to make it easy for them.

How does this affect the success of schemes to plant nesting cover? Planting huge blocks of nesting cover is all very well for the hens that end up nesting in them, but the hens will only do so if the cover is placed near to where the territories are. It may seem obvious but the money wasted by ignoring this simple fact is considerable. Rather than just taking whole fields and planting them with nesting cover, which is an expensive business, surely it makes more sense to spend a few mornings in April working out where the hens are likely to be and then planning to plant some nesting cover nearby for their benefit in subsequent years. It does not have to be huge blocks measured in hundreds of acres; strips 20–30 yards wide should be enough. Smaller strips than this tend to be too easy for predators to hunt along. Understanding nesting cover is certainly important, and the North Americans are masters at creating it. But without considering the hens' other needs and constraints it is all too easy to do it wrong.

HOW ATTRACTIVE ARE DIFFERENT TYPES OF COVER?

Given that the hens are limited in their choice of nest site by the fact that they are tied to the cocks' territories, what is the ideal sort of nesting cover they would choose?

There are numerous nesting studies to work with. People have gone out and searched areas of different habitat types to work out the density of nests, or they have radiotagged a sample of birds. From these we can get a pretty good picture of the hen's preferences and her likely chance of success. It is worth pointing out that studies based on nests just found by chance tend to give a very unbalanced picture of what happens. These people often just find the most exposed nests or those in habitats where people like to walk. They find a disproportionate number of nests in hedgerows or grassy strips, or destroyed nests in hayfields after cutting, and too few in dense habitats like nettle patches.

The picture that emerges is not particularly surprising, but it is very useful when it comes to providing the best sorts of nesting cover. When it comes to attractive nesting sites, strip cover such as hedgerows or fencelines, fields of lucerne or alfalfa (they are the same crop but the names differ in Europe and North America), tall, tussocky grasses left standing from the previous year and certain sorts of woodland are all good. Pasture, grain fields (at least early in the season), corn (maize) and other crops that are particularly bare in the spring are all bad. It is still worth bearing in mind, however, that some hens will nest almost anywhere. If there is no suitable cover near the cock's territory then the hens still have to nest somewhere and nests are frequently found in almost any crop or habitat type. If certain types of nesting cover were all that the hens were looking for in the spring then they would all nest in the good cover. But because they need cover near a territory and do not think ahead, we find a proportion of nests in unsuitable places simply because there was nothing better nearby. Hens will also end up in some pretty odd places. There are records of hens nesting up trees, particularly in old squirrel dreys, and I have even seen a photograph of a hen nesting in someone's kitchen sink!

The choice of preferred cover is not very surprising. Hens are coloured like dead grass for a good reason. They choose to lay eggs in cover that is relatively tall and provides cover and camouflage from predators. The interesting thing is that not all the crops that are attractive are safe. Alfalfa/lucerne is a case in point; although it is very attractive to nesting hens, it is usually cut for animal feed in the middle of the nesting season. Large numbers of nests, and often the hens as well, end up going through the mower. One

Hen pheasants are well camouflaged to blend in with dead grasses and leaves.

famous wild pheasant estate in the east of England claimed that the protein content of its harvested lucerne was only good because of the high proportion of pheasant hens and eggs included in the product! It is another example of the hen pheasant's lack of foresight; she chooses a nest site on the basis of the cover it provides, not the chances of her hatching off a clutch. Strip cover along hedgerows and fencelines is another example. Although these areas are among the most attractive to the birds, particularly in parts of American Midwest, where they provide about the only suitable nesting cover, they are not actually very good places to choose. Predators find it very easy to hunt along cover of this sort and the nests are particularly vulnerable. It seems as though the width of strip cover is one of the main factors in the vulnerability of the nests. A number of American studies suggest that wide strips are better than narrow ones, where many nests are lost. Increasing the width of strips from a few feet to a couple of yards can make a big difference.

Nesting studies can also be used to see which types of habitat are associated with high breeding densities. The areas rich in attractive nesting cover were not necessarily the ones that contained the most birds. A lot of strip cover makes for a lot of potential nest sites. But, based on the nesting studies, places with a lot of strip cover actually turned out to have some of the lowest breeding densities. Blocks of tall, residual grasses were good both for nesting and for achieving higher densities of birds, but these areas can act as both nest sites and as parts of territories in some areas, so putting this habitat's benefits down purely to nesting cover may be misleading. The one habitat that did come out as linked to high densities turned out to be shrubby cover. This can be good nesting cover but, as we saw in the previous chapter, it is also an important component of territories. This brings me back to the main message: nesting cover should be good, but unless the landscape also includes numerous sites for territories, it is not enough on its own to produce high densities of birds.

NEST SUCCESS

Despite stories of the number of nests that are lost to different causes, it is actually very difficult to get an objective picture of just how many nests go on to hatch and the reasons why so many do not. At first it may seem a simple operation: go out and find a lot of nests and see how many of them hatch. The trouble is that it is very hard to find nests just as they are started. Even with radiotelemetry it is often only possible to find them once the hen has started sitting. This can influence the results of the study, as nests that are already a long way into the process of being laid and incubated have already survived much of the danger period. It is a bit like asking how likely it is that someone will live to be a hundred: if you look at a group of five-year-olds, it is unlikely that any of them will reach that age; but if you only consider people who are already well into their

It is surprisingly difficult to get an accurate picture of hen pheasant breeding success by looking at the proportion of nests that hatch.
(John Carroll)

nineties then the chances are greater. Moreover, just going out looking for nests means that you tend to find those that are least well hidden, and if a human can find them then so probably can predators. This can be an even larger problem if nests exposed during hay or silage cutting are included. Almost by definition these nests have been destroyed, so it is very easy to get the impression that a high proportion of nests are lost in this way. All of this means that people tend to find the exposed nests when they have already gone quite a way towards hatching and it is very difficult to get an objective sample.

There are a number of studies that give the percentage of nests found that eventually hatch. The figure can vary from less than 10 per cent to over 60 per cent, depending on the area, the local level of predation, the density of hens and the quality of the cover. However, without a more detailed examination, none of these figures is particularly meaningful. In particular, each nest goes through two separate phases: the laying period when the hen only visits it occasionally to lay an egg; and the incubation period when she is actually sitting on the clutch. The extent of

Pheasant nests and sitting hens are particularly vulnerable to predators.

The fates of nests found in different habitat types, from a study by John Gates in Wisconsin in the early 1960s .

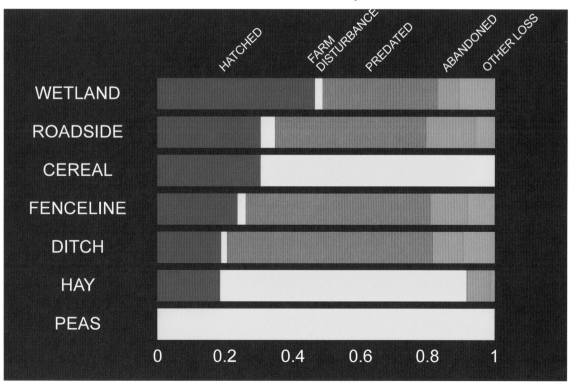

losses and the actual causes can vary quite considerably between the two.

In Britain, there are a number of schemes where members of the public or gamekeepers send in records of nests they happen to find. Although these suffer from the problem of bias I have already mentioned, they are recorded in enough detail to get a picture of how the losses vary between laying and incubation. During the laying period, losses are mainly due to predation by corvids (usually crows or magpies) or abandonment, the hen for some reason giving up the nest. Once the hen starts sitting, the causes of loss start to change. Predation by corvids and abandonment become much less prominent, while losses to mammalian predators, particularly foxes, increase. These differences are quite easy to explain. Crows of various sorts hunt by sight and are best at finding exposed eggs before the hen has covered them with her own body. The hen is also more likely to abandon a clutch during lay if she decides it is at risk before she has invested a lot of energy in it. Once she starts sitting, however, she has made a much greater commitment and the rate of abandonment falls. At this stage, nests also become more vulnerable to mammalian predators, which tend to hunt by scent as well as sight. A sitting hen may give off more scent than an unattended clutch of eggs.

How many of the nests that are started actually make it through to hatch? Again, this is not a particularly useful question because it varies considerably from place to place, and it is still a very hard thing to judge. The most objective information comes from radiotelemetry. But even here the nest may be made more vulnerable by the very fact that the hen is being radiotracked. Having a clumsy scientist poking through the vegetation cannot help the hen's chances of remaining secure – I must confess that I have even trodden on an incubating hen while looking for her nest. Moreover, the data from radiotracking only tends to cover the period of incubation. Bearing these things in mind, our records for Britain suggest that about 40 per cent of hens that start sitting on a clutch of eggs will see them through to hatch. Of course several more will have lost their eggs during lay, before we ever found them, and a 'guesstimate' of 20–30 per cent of nests surviving from the date the first egg was laid to hatch is probably not unreasonable.

The success rate of nests in different sorts of cover can also vary widely. From all the American nesting studies, a clear picture emerges. Hay fields are very attractive nesting sites but are dangerous, as many of the hens and nests are destroyed during cutting. As an example, John Gates, who located nearly 2,000 pheasant nests in Wisconsin in the 1960s found that nearly 70 per cent of those in hay fields were lost to farm operations and only 18 per cent hatched. Strip vegetation is also an attractive nesting habitat, but here the problem is predation. As I mentioned earlier these thin habitats seem to be very easy for predators to hunt along. The Wisconsin study again illustrates this. Along ditches or fencelines over 60 per cent of nests were lost to predators and 20–25 per cent hatched. On the wider roadside verges losses to predation were rather lower at 45 per cent and 30 per cent hatched. Unfarmed blocks of land, either the fringes of marshes, woodlands, reedbeds or fields of weeds and tussocky grasses are also attractive and are fairly safe places for nesting. They are too large for predators to search efficiently as they do along fencerows, and they are not disturbed by the farmers. John Gates found that the edges of wetlands were the most successful areas for pheasant nesting: almost 50 per cent of nests hatched with 36 per cent lost to predation. Apart from hay fields, other agricultural crops are not attractive to nesting pheasants; corn (maize) fields, soya and the like are particularly poor. Cereals and peas can attract low numbers of nesting birds, although here again farming activities cause problems. In Wisconsin, every nest in pea fields was destroyed during harvesting while the farm operations also accounted for 70 per cent of those in cereals. However, in the cereals 30 per cent of nests did hatch. If they were not destroyed by the farmer then they were fairly safe from predators.

While these sorts of study are good when it comes to comparing different crops, they are not so reliable when it comes to working out the overall breeding success of a population. To start with, the hens will often lay a second, third or even fourth nest if they lose their first. They may also renest after hatching a brood of chicks that all die within a few days. Lastly, the figures for nest success are unreliable. I have more faith in looking at the proportion of hens that actually end up with a brood of chicks at the end of the season as a measure of breeding success. Because we often know how many hens are in an area in April, we can use the number of broods we find in August as a measure of how many of the hens actually succeed. There are also a large number of other published studies that can be used, and these give us a much more reliable picture of breeding success than I think we will ever achieve from simply recording the fate of individual nests.

BREEDING SUCCESS

Getting to grips with how pheasant breeding success varies in different areas and different years is a complex business. One has to get a good count of the number of hens on a piece of land in the spring and then the number and sizes of the broods at the end of the summer. Fortunately, these are the sorts of figures that can be found in many scientific publications, stretching back to the 1930s. We have been able to put together over 70 sets of figures to see how breeding success varies. The range is enormous: one of our own studies of released birds found that 100 hens alive in the spring failed to fledge a single chick, while at the other extreme, some American workers record 100 hens in spring leading to nearly 700 chicks at the end of the summer. Why should there be such an enormous variation?

When we take a closer look at what is happening, a number of different trends appear. First, breeding stocks in those areas where birds are released seem to have particular problems, and this is the subject of a later chapter. In studies of wild pheasant populations, there is a clear link between the density of hens in spring and their breeding success. Where the hens are thinly spread they each seem to do particularly well. The studies where 100 hens produced 700 chicks were all low-density populations of around three hens per 100 acres. As hen density increases, so their individual breeding success falls. At ten hens per 100 acres, fledging falls to around 300 chicks per 100 hens. When breeding density rises to 25 hens per 100 acres, production again falls, to an average of 150 chicks per 100 hens. At really high spring hen densities of 50 hens per 100 acres, 100 hens only fledge 80 chicks. The

obvious conclusion is therefore that hens do best at low densities and their individual chances of fledging chicks fall off rapidly as densities increase. Why should this be the case?

One thing that can be ruled out is a variation in chick survival. If this were the cause we would expect to see smaller broods in populations at high densities, whereas there is no clear pattern of chick survival between high- and low-density populations. What does seem to be happening is that at high densities more hens seem to die during the breeding season and more of the survivors end up with no chicks, presumably because they have lost their nests. If we are to understand why productivity is so closely linked to density we should really be asking why hen and nest loss changes in relation to population density.

One clue comes from studies on islands with limited numbers of predators or areas where gamekeepers have reduced predator numbers. In these places the link between hen density and breeding success vanishes. Under these conditions 100 wild hens seem to be able to fledge 400–600 chicks, regardless of density. In areas with limited predator populations it seems as though hen survival and nest success remain high, regardless of bird density. Could it be that predators are the cause of the link between breeding success and density in other areas? The circumstantial evidence is strong. When prey is abundant it pays an adaptable predator to become a specialist in hunting it or finding its nests. However, what is really needed is an experiment to see what happens when the predators are removed and everything else is kept constant. Unfortunately this has never been done properly for pheasants. The best study I know of was not carried out on pheasants, but on the grey partridge. I will say more about this study later, but it clearly showed the link between predation and the productivity of this species. Once the predators were removed, hen partridge survival and breeding success increased, and the density effect disappeared. Partridge are fairly similar to pheasants and their populations show the same sort of density effects on breeding success as I have described for pheasants, but only where predators are present in unrestricted numbers. The experimental control of predators and their effects on partridge breeding success show that

The chances of a hen pheasant alive in spring going on to successfully rear a brood of chicks seems to be affected by the density of pheasants in the area.

predators are almost certainly a major cause of the link between production and density in pheasants.

Is this really important? The answer is very clearly yes. If we want to see more wild pheasants in the autumn we need to know what limits their numbers. While habitat can control the density of birds that try to breed in an area, hunters also want to see those birds produce a lot of chicks so that there is a healthy autumn stock that can be harvested. If predation is limiting the ability of hens to produce broods and this effect becomes more and more pronounced as breeding density increases, then it can severely curtail production.

To get an idea of how important this effect is, think of each hen pheasant in the spring as money invested in the bank. In an ideal world each would fledge a brood of chicks – think of them as the interest on the investment. The idea is to take that interest and spend it – equivalent to hunting. What predation does is to tax the interest, and the tax rate increases rapidly according to the size of the investment. When the investment is small (where there is a low-density breeding population), then the tax is really very small: it is hardly worth the tax man bothering to collect it (i.e. the predators do not key in to pheasants as an important food resource). However, when the investment is large, the tax can be huge, greater than 100 per cent in many cases, which means one ends up with less money than one started with. The investor is fighting a losing battle – every time things go well the tax man takes so much that the investor is pushed back down again. If one wants to enjoy a really high rate of interest the thing to do is either avoid the tax man or get rid of him. So to achieve the highest pheasant densities, predation must be controlled in some way. This is not just so that the population will produce a large annual surplus of young, but also so that there is scope for the population to increase in the future.

This discussion of predators is by necessity an oversimplification. It is not just during the nesting season that pheasants suffer losses, and the other losses are not always linked to density or predation. For instance, to achieve high autumn numbers and a healthy population that has the potential to increase, the chicks also need to grow and survive. Chick survival is affected by many things quite unrelated to bird density or predation, but no less important. These are the subject of the next chapter.

CHICKS

Once the eggs hatch the most critical time in the pheasant's year begins. More pheasants die as young chicks than at any other time of the year and chick survival seems to be one of the most critical factors in deciding how many birds will be around in the autumn. An average nest will contain about 11 eggs, of which nine will probably hatch. Within two or three weeks this brood of nine will typically dwindle to half or less of its original size. In other words, half of the pheasants ever hatched die in their first few weeks of life.

Chicks are incredibly vulnerable during their first few days and conditions must be just right if a good number of them are to survive. In the 1930s and 1940s everything seemed to be in their favour. Providing the weather was reasonably dry, large broods of pheasants were a common sight throughout Europe and North America. However, something has gone drastically wrong. Across vast areas of land the number of chicks

The first few weeks are the most dangerous part of a pheasant's life.

surviving to fledge has gradually dwindled, not just among pheasants but also among partridges. What can be the cause of so many chicks dying across whole continents year after year?

One suggestion that is often made is that pheasants are bad mothers, willing to leave their chicks at the slightest excuse. Hen pheasants are certainly not renowned as good parents but they can, on occasion, be perfect mothers. I have twice seen hens carrying out distraction displays to divert me from the young chicks hiding nearby. On both occasions the hen pretended to be wounded, dragging one wing along the ground as if it were broken. If I had been a predator the chances are I would have followed the hen in the hope of an easy meal rather than searching for the vulnerable chicks. By risking her own life the hen was hoping to prevent me finding her young.

Radiotracking has shown us that hen pheasants are often better mothers than many people imagine.

One of the advantages of radiotelemetry is the insight it gives into the behaviour of the birds, and this can lay to rest some of the misconceptions about the mothering ability of the hen pheasant. When we approach a hen with a young brood of chicks it is quite normal for her to leave the chicks and go running off, directly away from us. At first sight this may seem a very selfish approach, and not good maternal behaviour. However, because we can follow the hen with our equipment we know that she usually runs about 50 yards and then circles around to return to the chicks from a different direction. While it may seem that she has abandoned the brood, she is in fact waiting nearby for the opportunity to return.

Hens will also do more than just try to distract attention from the chicks; they will fight back against predators that attack their young. John Carroll, who was working on pheasants in North Dakota in the 1980s, twice saw hens fight off northern harriers (the same species as European hen harriers) which were attacking their broods. These harriers are not big enough to kill an adult pheasant but will certainly take partially grown chicks or poults. John saw a hen flying straight at a harrier that was circling over her brood, apparently hitting it in mid-air with her wings and feet. Another American worker even saw groups of cock pheasants repeatedly attacking harriers feeding on half-grown poults. When pheasants are not themselves at risk of being killed by the predator, they seem quite willing to turn and defend their chicks.

I also wonder whether hens will sometimes kill small ground predators that attack the nest. The British Trust for Ornithology collects records of nests found by interested birdwatchers each year. They have about 1,500 of these for pheasants over the last 40 years and in two cases they include accounts of nests with dead stoats. Did the hens kill them as they came too close? Certainly two accounts is suggestive. I doubt whether we will ever know for sure, but nesting hens are certainly far more aggressive than normal.

All in all, I think that the maternal nature of the typical hen has been underestimated. Although she will often run away from her chicks if disturbed, this is not desertion. She will be back when the danger has gone and often try to divert the potential predator away from the brood. This is not to say that hen pheasants are perfect mothers – far from it – simply that their skills are easily underestimated. Furthermore, when it comes to trying to explain long-term declines in chick survival, one cannot blame maternal care. They were once able to raise big broods, so why should this have changed?

Weather is one possibile explanation for poor chick survival. Those with an interest in game have long known that fairly dry weather during the period when most chicks hatch bodes well for the next shooting season, and lots of healthy chicks means a good autumn population for the hunt. In fact, in the case of partridges, this has led to a piece of folklore: if the sun is shining during the annual horseracing meeting at Royal Ascot in Berkshire then it will be a good year for shooting. There is certainly some truth in this, as there is without doubt a trend for warm summers to produce more chicks. A quick look at any set of bag records for wild pheasants in England clearly shows peak numbers in the warm summers of the early 1960s and mid-1970s. So is weather then to blame for the long-term declines in chick survival that have occurred since the 1930s and 1940s? It cannot be, as there is no evidence that our summers have become colder and wetter. Even if this were the case in some areas, it does not hold true across the continents, and chicks are dying almost everywhere. And although a sudden decline in numbers often corresponds to a series of wet summers, these have often occurred in the past, but previously numbers have recovered when warm summers have come around again. Nowadays game numbers seem to stay low and any recoveries are fairly modest. There is no doubt that weather has a big effect and is without doubt a major cause of year-to-year changes in the number of chicks fledged, but what it cannot explain is why there have been long-term declines or why, in years with similarly good weather, our hens now produce fewer grown poults.

Changes in the amount of habitat available is another possible reason, and it is without doubt an important consideration for the size of many populations, but can it explain why there are fewer chicks? The loss of winter cover, food sources, territory sites and nesting cover will all lead to a reduction in the number of pheasants. But although they may lead to fewer nesting hens and fewer chicks being hatched, it is hard to see how they could lead to the chicks dying. Of course, there are areas where there has been a radical shift in the sorts of crops grown. In some parts of Illinois pheasant chick survival dropped as more areas were planted up with maize as opposed to other cereals. Things like this can be very important, but only on a local basis. There are many parts of the world where chicks have been dying, even though the basic agricultural crops have remained the same. Just like the weather, habitat loss is an important factor for pheasants but cannot be the culprit when it comes to killing chicks in so many different places.

The hens may be less well fed or sickening for some reason. Perhaps pesticides have reduced the fertility of their eggs. Could there be something affecting the number of eggs they lay or their viability? All of these can be quickly discounted. Pheasant nests contain the same numbers of eggs as they did between the two world wars and hatchability has remained unchanged.

Predators are another possibility — it is not hard to imagine how more searching eyes and hungry mouths would lead to fewer chicks. Increased predation, not just of chicks but also of eggs, can mean smaller broods. If a hen loses her first clutch to an egg predator she will usually go on to lay a second, sometimes a third or very rarely a fourth. These replacement clutches become progressively smaller and, if they manage to hatch, will obviously produce fewer chicks. Predation could therefore explain the long-term changes. In North America, where there is little in the way of predator control, it is hard to find evidence to test whether this really is the case, but in Britain predator control has a long history and is an integral part of wild pheasant management in many areas. If widespread increases in predators were the problem with our chicks then British wild pheasant or partridge estates with gamekeepers, whose main job it is to keep predator numbers down, should have been relatively immune to the problem. Unfortunately, if anything British farms have suffered greater declines in chick survival than in other countries. As with all the other factors mentioned, predators may be part of the story,

Warm dry summers seem to produce the largest number of pheasant chicks.

Although predators are an important part of the pheasant life, they do not seem to be the cause of declining chick survival in many areas. (Jonathan Reynolds)

but something else is happening.

Since none of the obvious possibilities seem to provide an explanation, what do we know about the early life of the pheasant that might help explain the problems the chicks are facing? After they hatch, the chicks tend to stay under the hen for the first night while they dry and prepare to leave the nest. At hatch the chicks have not used up all the yolk that they used to grow inside the egg. They keep a store of it inside themselves for the first day or two and can use this rather than feeding. This does not last long, however, and on the day after hatch the hen leads them away from the nest to feed. She does not seem to have planned where she is going to take the chicks. When we have followed hens with radiotracking, they just seem to walk at random until they find a suitable area. They will often pass near to ideal sites only to end up in some unsuitable place. During all of this time the chicks run along behind the hen. For the first week or two they are too small to heat their own bodies and, when they start to chill, they must get under the hen to be brooded. This is particularly important if the weather is cold or if they have to move through damp vegetation.

84

Until biologists had radiotracking to help them, the only way to get an idea of chick diet was to catch chicks and kill them to find out what they had been eating. Thankfully, we have never had to do that and radiotracking allows us to find out where the hen roosts with the chicks underneath her. We go out at night and mark the position of the brood without getting too close. This is not always as simple as it sounds, following a bleeping electronic box around a farm in the dark. Especially if the rendezvous for those going out that night has been a warm country pub, it can be a fairly disorientating experience! On one occasion I found that I had accurately marked out the position of an electric fence whose pulses sounded just like the signal from a radio. Ditches are also always twice as wide if they have to be jumped at night.

In the morning we go back and search the ground for signs of the roost, usually a flattened area with a circle of droppings. These droppings can tell us all we need to know about the diet of

To understand chick diet we search for roost sites and collect the chick droppings for later analysis.

the chicks. Insects and seeds are not completely digested as they pass through the gut. By washing the droppings through a fine sieve we can separate out the remaining pieces and try to put them back together to find out what the chicks had eaten. It is a laborious business but not quite as bad as it sounds. Many insects leave characteristic traces, the heads of caterpillars, legs of beetles and, for some strange reason, the reproductive organs of spiders, are all readily identifiable if one knows what to look for. Steve Moreby at the Game Conservancy Trust has made this his life's work and is annually supplied with small tubes of assorted droppings. In this way we can literally piece together their diet without even having to see the chicks, let alone catch them.

These studies show us a number of things. First, the chicks feed on almost nothing but insects until they are a week old. After that they start to include seeds and other green matter, but insects still form the largest part of their diet until they are quite well grown. The advantage of insects is that they are a very rich source of protein, particularly animal protein which contains specific amino acids needed for growing

Sampling the insects within the chicks feeding range lets us monitor how food availability affects survival, although the D-vac suction samplers we use can be rather cumbersome.

feathers amongst other things. Studies of captive chicks fed different diets has clearly shown that a high protein content in their diet is vital if they are to grow and be able to withstand stresses such as cold weather and rain. The chicks are also selective about which sorts of insects they feed on, partly because some are easier to catch, but also because some are more nutritious than others.

Radiotracking enables us to discover where the chicks are taken to feed. We can then sample the insects found in those areas to see which occur most often in the diet. The chicks feed on quite a specific group of large, slow-moving insects that are found near ground level: certain beetles, plant bugs, caterpillars and sawfly larvae. Other groups like flies and aphids are rarely eaten, even though they are often the most common groups in the area. So just because an area is full of insects, it does not mean it will be a good hunting ground for the chicks; they must be of the right sort.

Radiotracking also enables us to discover

which habitats the chicks use. By finding their location every few hours we can discover whether there are some places they prefer and others they avoid. From this it is clear that they like the edges of cereal fields, rough grass and weedy areas. They avoid woodlands, maize fields, short grass and rape. These preferences also correspond to the richness of the areas in insects. Weedy areas often contain five times as many insects as maize.

Plant bugs are a preferred food item for young pheasant chicks. (Nick Sotherton)

chicks prefer. If a high proportion of the chicks that hatch are to survive it seems that they need a rich supply of the right sort of insects on which to feed.

So could the decline in chick survival be due to changes in the availability of insects in cereal fields? What has happened to farmland throughout Europe and North America since the 1930s and 1940s that might have influenced the insects it contains? Put like this the answer is fairly obvious. Farming methods have changed out of all recognition since the Second World War. Not only have the crops changed but there is hardly

This information on the pheasant's early life throws up a number of new ideas about why chicks are dying. We know that the chicks need insects if they are to thrive, we know that they are fussy about which sorts of insects they eat, and we know that they concentrate their time in cereal fields and weedy areas. We have followed about 30 broods through their early life with the aid of radiotracking and a number of pictures have emerged. Chicks that survive well do not tend to move around very much, concentrating their time in small areas for the first week or so of life. This makes sense, as moving around all the time uses energy that could otherwise be used to grow flesh and bones. The areas where successful chicks concentrate their time are also particularly rich in insects, especially those groups that we know the

a crop that is not now sprayed with insecticides or herbicides, not to mention the fungicides and fertilisers that go with them. In Britain at least, it was seen as a matter of national security to increase the quantity of homegrown food after the U-boat blockade in the early 1940s. Money was poured into farming to raise production, while advances in pesticides and crop strains have produced yields impossible only a few decades ago. Farmers rose to the challenge and did exactly what various governments wanted, but there has been a cost. Apart from the fact that we no longer need all the subsidised farming products that we produce, the ecological changes on farmland have been profound. Weeds which were once a characteristic part of the country scene fell into decline. Shepherd's needle, and a

The more intensive use of pesticides has led to declines in many of the weeds and insects once found in cereal fields, although new techniques such as Conservation Headlands, where reduced pesticides are applied to the field edge, can help alleviate the problem. (Nick Sotherton)

host of other plants associated with cereal fields were once important agricultural pests. This plant was once so common that whole fields were left unharvested because of infestation, but it is now among the most endangered plants found in Britain.

By 1950 some 15 per cent of British cereals received an application of herbicide, rising to 63 per cent in 1960. It is now virtually unknown for a crop to remain unsprayed. This trend has been repeated throughout Europe and, to a lesser extent, in North America, with the main increases occurring between 1955 and 1975.

Removing weeds from farmland may not seem to affect insect food for pheasant chicks directly. Fewer weeds may mean fewer seeds for the chicks, but as we have seen they concentrate on insects, so declining weed seeds should not be of much importance. However, throughout the 1960s and 1970s it became increasingly clear that removing weeds led to a direct reduction in the abundance of insects. Relatively few insects actually feed on growing crops and those pest species that do tend to be the ones that young chicks do not feed on, aphids being an obvious example. The vast majority of the insects that pheasant chicks eat live on weeds. Remove the weeds and the insects are gone. Insecticides certainly contribute to the problem, but herbicides seem to be the main culprit.

But have herbicides really been the cause of the declines in chick survival? In the 1980s a team at the Game Conservancy Trust called the Cereals and Gamebirds Project set out to test these ideas. They developed ways of combining the insects that gamebird chicks need with productive farming methods. Led by Dick Potts' work on partridges, Nick Sotherton and his team set out to discover just how pesticides might be affecting chick survival.

Their approach was, at first sight, very simple. They asked a number of co-operative land-owners to leave the edges of their fields unsprayed and then compared the survival of pheasant and partridge chicks in these areas with neighbouring, fully sprayed fields. At the same time they recorded the weed growth along sprayed and unsprayed field edges and sampled the numbers of insects. Hugh Oliver-Bellasis, the co-owner of the Manydown Estate on the outskirts of Basingstoke to the west of London, was Chairman of the Cereals and Gamebirds Project and was the first to try out the idea. He has a special passion for partridges and was particularly keen to try to restore his stocks, which had dwindled to a fraction of their former numbers. Things went well. In the absence of herbicides and insecticides the number of weeds along the crop edge increased. So too did the populations of insects, and partridge and pheasant chick survival was doubled, bringing levels back up to those found before the advent of modern farming. In terms of proving that pesticides were at the root of the problem for young gamebirds the first few years of the project were a resounding success.

However, if Conservation Headlands, as the treating of the outer 6m of a field with fewer chemicals became known, were to be widely adopted by farmers, it was vital to make sure that they would not lead to significant weed problems. A scattering of small weeds is not a problem for a farmer, particularly at the edge of the field where the crop does not usually grow well anyway. But a serious weed infestation spreading into the main bulk of the crop is another matter.

Conservation Headlands reduce the use of pesticides around the edge of the field, allowing many flowers and chick food insects to survive. (Nick Sotherton)

After identifying pesticides as the problem, the team had to try and find out which ones were especially to blame. Which ones were relatively benign to gamebirds and their food, but would still kill the important agricultural weeds? There was no point in solving the problem if farmers were not going to do anything about it.

This led to the largest part of the project's work, going through the huge list of chemicals that farmers apply to their fields and identifying which should be used and which should not. Eventually, after four or five years of trials, the project produced its recommendations. These cleared almost all of the fungicides, all growth promoters, certain insecticides and a range of herbicides that were found to kill only grasses, not the small broad-leaved weeds that turned out to be particularly important for insects. There is now a comprehensive list of chemicals which can be used to protect the crop while still leaving enough food for the chicks. Their recommendations have also been fully costed and the price is negligible.

Regularly cut set-aside can be a disaster for game. (Nick Sotherton)

The problems with Conservation Headlands are mainly to do with the management skills necessary to ensure that the right chemicals are applied to the right part of the field. Their introduction also came shortly before the advent of set-aside as part of the British farming scene. It requires a careful manager to ensure that tractor drivers, who may not care about gamebird chicks, are fully informed and take the time to treat the field edges in a separate way from the rest of the field. Many farms found that getting it right was just too much of a problem. The introduction of compulsory set-aside was another blow. While many farmers might have been willing to compromise production on a small proportion of their land, if they had also to take a large area out of cereal production as set-aside then they often wanted to farm the remainder as intensively as possible. Conservation Headlands were designed to have as little impact on grain production as possible, while set-aside aimed to have as large an effect as possible to reduce yields and surplus production. The two just did not go together in most farmers' minds.

Despite these problems the effects of Conservation Headlands should not be underestimated. They provide a practical and cost-effective method of restoring chick survival rates to pre-war levels and clearly demonstrate the importance of pesticides to the chicks' food supplies. Not only can they increase and often double the sizes of the broods, they also lead to more butterflies, wild flowers, small mammals and insect life in general. As a practical demonstration of what can be done to integrate game management, conservation and productive farming, they are surely unsurpassed.

Set-aside in Britain provided a huge opportunity for game, but in the first few years it was a disaster. The Government was keen to see a scheme that was easily monitored and would keep the land in a condition where it could easily be brought back into production should the need arise. For the first few years of the scheme the

only real option was to let a field revert to grass and mow it a couple of times during the year – an absolute disaster for game. The only thing these fields provided was food during the winter and nesting cover. Winter food is good but is not really essential in Britain. And while nesting cover is a good thing, the regulations virtually ensured that the grass was cut at the height of the nesting season, killing many of the birds attempting to nest in it.

At the end of the 1980s, I had the chance to visit Austria, at that time outside the European Community, and visited the Seefeld Estate. The Austrian government had its own version of set-aside, a far more flexible scheme than anything Brussels had allowed. Rather than monotonous fields of mown grass, the owners of Seefeld were planting mixes of cereals and various broad-leaved crops such as rape, kale, sunflowers and lucerne (alfalfa). These were similar to the weedy cereal fields we were trying to create with

Many hens are killed by cutting in set-aside fields during the nesting season. (Nick Sotherton)

Cereal mix set-aside can provide ideal brood habitat for young pheasants.

Conservation Headlands, and the Austrian regulations did not require these pieces of set-aside to be cut. As a consequence they provided ideal conditions for pheasant nesting and chick production, and the estate held some spectacular wild pheasant densities. Karl Pock, the gamekeeper at Seefeld, agreed to count pheasant broods on the estate. He found that broods of pheasant chicks in or near to the set-aside fields averaged about six and a half chicks per hen, compared to only three or four in those broods in more typical and fully sprayed cereal fields. This came as a real eye-opener for me. On my return to the Game Conservancy Trust, I bored all my colleagues with my accounts of how wonderful Austrian set-aside was. This was about the limit of my contribution to the set-aside debate, but others in the Game Conservancy held similar views and their research and lobbying eventually led to the acceptance of unharvested cereal mixes as a valid use of set-aside land. This is currently allowed under the Wild Bird Cover Option, and a very good thing too.

Weedy cereal fields, whether from the low-input agriculture seen before the Second World War, Conservation Headlands or cereal mix set-aside, are obviously not the only habitats that are good for chicks. There must be others, such as the ones which they evolved in China, that can provide the same things. In North America there are studies that find very good chick survival in what they call old fields, areas that have been abandoned by farmers and have reverted to a mix of grasses and weeds. When I first heard of these studies I found it hard to visualise what these areas might look like; in Britain such fields would soon become dense and wet, poor places for a hen to try and rear a brood. The thing I had forgotten was the much lower rainfall in many parts of North America compared to Britain. When I had the chance to see some of these old fields things became clearer. Rather than a dense sward of solid grass they were actually quite open, with room for the chicks to move around and search for insects. Grass fields in dry climates or on poor soils can provide a structure rather similar to a thin cereal crop, and the chicks love them in just the same way.

With all the variations in climate throughout

the pheasant's world-wide range it is very difficult to provide recipes for the type of vegetation which will be best for the chicks. However, it is probably true that they need three things if they are to thrive in an area, and I suspect that these are much the same anywhere. The first is obviously insects, as without these they stand little chance of survival. The insects must be the right sort – slow-moving creatures living near the bottom of the crop. But insects alone are not enough.

There are many habitats which provide many of these sorts of insects, but are still death-traps to very young pheasants. The second thing the chicks need is ease of movement through the crop. If it is very dense at ground level then the chicks will struggle to get through it and, in even moderately wet climates, they risk becoming waterlogged and dying of exposure.

Lastly, they must have concealment from predators. We once tried introducing tame chicks to different crop types to examine their feeding rates. We obviously only did this when the crops were dry and the chicks were at no risk, and we expected to find that their feeding rate would closely match the number of insects available for them to eat. What emerged was broadly in line with what we expected, with the exception of crops where the chicks had very poor overhead cover. In these habitats, short, herb-rich grassland in particular, the chicks just did not seem to want to feed. They either spent all their time looking about nervously or crouching in the corner of the cages, and in my opinion they were too scared to feed. A study of the places we know the hen actually takes the chicks in the wild confirms this. It is very rare to find a brood in a habitat that does not provide cover over their heads, even if it is one that is very rich in insects. The chicks certainly need to feed on insects but it must be in a crop that allows them freedom of movement and one where they are hidden from view.

THE WEATHER

We have seen that weather is unlikely to be the reason for the long-term declines in pheasant chick survival. This is not to say it is unimportant – it is the main reason why some years are good and some are bad – it is just that it cannot explain long-term trends. It is also too easy to see the effects of the weather as an Act of God and assume that there is nothing that can be done about it. All to often, gamekeepers and managers shrug their shoulders and say, 'How could we expect to have many birds after such a bad summer?'

Modern farmland can be an inhospitable habitat for small chicks.

This approach to the weather can be very dangerous and almost denied me the chance to work on pheasants as a career. The Game Conservancy Trust, was once part of ICI, the chemical company. ICI held a virtual monopoly on the manufacture of shotgun cartridges in Britain in the middle of this century. The Eley Game Research Association, as the Game Conservancy Trust was then called, was funded by the company to ensure that game populations remained healthy and cartridge sales were high. In the 1960s the company went through a massive reorganisation and brought in Lord Beeching to rationalise its structure. His hard-headed approach to business and the wasteful use of resources became more obvious in his later job of reorganising the British railway system. He arrived at our headquarters in Fordingbridge and his first question was, 'Why do all the game populations (and cartridge sales) vary so much from year to year?' The answer given was 'the weather.' 'Well, all the research in the world can't do much about that', he said. The funding was withdrawn and the research side of the organisation came very close to folding. As with so much in research, the key is not in the answer, but in getting the question right in the first place. Rephrasing the question as 'Why are the birds so sensitive to the weather and what can be done to reduce its effects?', opens up all sorts of possibilities. (To be fair to Lord Beeching it is probable that the funding would have been cut in any case as the company was losing its monopoly on cartridge sales to foreign imports.)

So how does the weather affect the survival of the chicks? The link between the weather at the time when the chicks hatch and their subsequent survival has long been appreciated. Wet weather, and the sudden heavy thunderstorms so characteristic of the British climate at that time of year, certainly kill chicks. Furthermore, the survival of the young during their first few days of life is undoubtedly one of the main factors affecting the size of the stock in the autumn.

Britain rarely experiences hot, dry summers but too little rain can also be a problem. At Seefeld in Austria, there is a clear link between the numbers shot and the weather in the previous summer. Poor shooting seasons are not just associated with wet weather, but also with excessively dry years. The pheasants only seem to thrive when there is a bit of rain but not too much, and I think the same is also true across much of North America.

The weather kills chicks in two ways. When they first hatch they cannot keep themselves warm and must be brooded by the hen every now and then to keep warm. If the weather is cold they need more attention from the hen and can spend less time feeding. A sudden drenching with cold rain can also kill them outright, while struggling through dank, wet vegetation can have the same effect. This is fairly obvious, but is only part of the story. For instance, it does not explain why hot weather can also be a problem. This brings us to the second factor: food.

Insects such as this sawfly larva, form a vital part of the diet of young pheasant chicks. (Nick Sotherton)

For their first week or two of life the chicks feed almost exclusively on large, slow-moving insects. As I mentioned earlier, most of these are found on the weeds that grow amongst agricultural crops. Insects are also influenced by the weather: cold, wet weather means fewer insects while hot, dry conditions mean fewer juicy weeds and therefore also fewer insects feeding on them. Indeed, instead of relying on the weather during Royal Ascot, one of our game advisers judges the hunting prospects by how often he has to clean the insects from his car's windscreen – a more direct method of assessing the same thing.

Direct losses of chicks to cold rain and a shortage of food are closely linked. Richard

Warner, a biologist from Illinois, has found a connection between the diet of young chicks and their vulnerability to cold rain. Well-fed chicks can survive such weather much better than half-starved ones. A miserable summer means little food and also poorly-fed chicks that are more vulnerable to the weather.

Can anything be done to solve this problem? The answer is a very definite yes. Two things are required: first, make sure they are well-fed and secondly, stop them from getting wet.

Feeding the chicks is a matter of choosing the right crops and being careful with the pesticides. I have already described how this can be done, but remember that a well-fed chick is much more robust than a half-starved one and better able to cope with what the weather throws at it.

Keeping the chicks dry is not as strange an idea as it sounds. I am not suggesting covering the countryside with pheasant shelters: the chicks can hopefully hide under the hen when it is actually raining. The problem comes when they try to move through the vegetation when it is still wet. Anyone who has walked through a crop of wheat or long grass after a rainstorm can vouch for the amount of water it can hold – when I was radio-tracking in Ireland I took to wearing a pair of waist-length wading boots if I had to go into an even slightly wet crop – so one can imagine the effects on a chick no more than a few days old. Certain crops hold more water at ground level than others, dense crops or those with low leaves are particularly bad in this respect. I am sure that this is the reason why British pheasant chicks like to feed in cereal fields but not in dense grass, even though the latter may contain more insects. I could never understand why so many North American biologists regarded grassy areas as being good for pheasant chicks until I saw them. In their drier summers, moisture retention is not such a problem and the grasses tend to be quite sparse, not like the rank British fields at all. Of course the birds can feed safely in dense crops if the weather is dry, but the trend in modern farming to have larger and larger fields means that the birds can no longer choose where to feed and must make do with what is available. The mixture of sparse, diverse crops found before modern farming technology took over meant a wealth of open and dense areas for feeding, with sunlit drying areas in between. This has now been lost and they must make do with what is left.

If a habitat is too dense at ground level or, as in this case, provides little in the way of a protective canopy, it will not prove to be a good site for young pheasant chicks to forage.

Do these ideas actually work? It is important to realise that all the care in the world will not stop birds dying in bad weather, but it will mean that fewer succumb. At Seefeld in Austria, modern agricultural techniques were introduced in the mid-1970s, including the widespread use of pesticides and a switch to large, uniform areas of single crops. A detailed look at the number of birds they shot in relation to the weather shows that, both before and after 1975, very wet or dry summers produced fewer birds than those with more moderate weather. However, since 1975 the effects have been much more severe. Given the same weather conditions, they now shoot fewer birds than they would have in previous years. Modern farming has made the birds more vulnerable to the weather and it now has a more important role than when the chicks could find food in abundance. The weather is, on average, the same now as it was 20 years ago, but changes in farming have made the difference. Summer weather will still lead to year-to-year changes in bird numbers, but instead of making the differ-ence between a good and a moderate year for shooting, it now makes the difference between a moderate and a poor year. Hopefully this situa-tion is changing as they plant more of their cereal-mix set-aside, but only time will tell.

Conversely, those farmers that have started using Conservation Headlands, the technique of being selective with the pesticides at the edge of the field, produce more chicks than their neigh-bours who spray indiscriminately, regardless of the weather. Of course there are still good and bad years, but the good ones are better, and the bad ones not so disastrous. The weather will always be there and will make managing game populations somewhat unpredictable, but it is something that can be planned for. The trick is to manage the habitats in which the chicks will feed, providing them with a rich insect food supply, the ability to move freely without becoming water-logged, and overhead protection from predators. Lord Beeching got the wrong answer to the wrong question.

REARING AND RELEASE

T he history of rearing pheasants is probably as old as their introduction to Europe. The first few birds were almost certainly kept in semi-captivity and the Romans have left us accounts of how to cage and keep them. One of the main reasons for the spectacular success of the pheasant is the ease with which it can be reared. Its close relative the chicken has long been a domestic animal, and pheasant eggs can readily be incubated and reared under broody hens. The ease with which this can be done has made rearing pheasants a part of their management since there was a demand for more birds, whether for hunting, the table or just aesthetics.

Pheasant rearing has a long history and can greatly increase bird densities, at least for a while.

Rearing and releasing can serve a number of different purposes. The spread of pheasants across Europe and North America has depended on rearing, in part, to provide the initial stocks of birds on the ground. Rearing and releasing to establish new populations has obviously been a great success. Rearing has also long been a popular way of increasing the numbers of birds in an area. Hunters want more birds and rearing has often been a successful way of meeting this need, although it can be expensive. However, rearing is also seen as a way of bolstering a declining wild stock and here, as we shall see, the results are decidedly mixed.

It is worth bearing in mind these three different aims: seeding a new population, increasing the number of birds available for shooting and trying to increase the natural production of a population. They are often confused, they require

Pheasants chicks can be reared under broody hens. (Hugo Straker)

entirely different methods, and they have very different levels of success. Large amounts of money have been wasted by confusing these separate aims of pheasant release. However, before we can examine the successes and failures of rearing and release it is worth looking at the actual mechanics of producing the birds in the first place.

REARING SYSTEMS

Rearing has come a long way since its early beginnings. Nowadays probably 50 million pheasants are reared world-wide for release. This amounts to almost the same number as are shot each year in Europe and North America. Pheasant rearing has become an industry in itself, employing gamekeepers, game farmers and specialist feed manufacturers, and in the process, supporting many of the staff at the Game Conservancy Trust. The successes and failures of pheasant rearing also gave me my first introduction to the subject of game management: my doctorate set out to determine the success of releases in southern Ireland and to assess their contribution to the resident stock.

Pheasants differ from chickens in that they are not particularly adept at incubating their eggs or rearing chicks in captivity. Although captive hen pheasants will happily lay eggs, the different rearing systems developed over the years usually rely on other means of incubating them. For many years the basic system was to collect eggs, either from wild pheasant nests or from captive hens in laying pens, and to place them under a broody domestic chicken for incubation. These broodies incubate the eggs as if they were their own, and will then brood the chicks after hatch. Early rearing systems started by replacing the foster mother's own eggs with those of the pheasant and letting her rear the chicks in a semi-wild condition. This was later intensified to the point where the bantam was kept in a small pen or coop with a slatted entrance. This open-field rearing system allowed the chicks to run freely in and out to feed and be brooded, but kept the hen in one place. It was the first system used on an intensive basis by British gamekeepers in the mid-1800s, when driven pheasant shooting first became fashionable. It was labour intensive, with numerous small coops, each containing a chicken with her brood of chicks. Food had to be provided for them all, according to complex recipes to ensure a high protein diet. Each game-keeper had his own favourite, with special ingredients such as ant larvae or boiled eggs. Each night at dusk the chicks had to be shepherded back into the coops to be brooded and the doors closed until the following morning. When the chicks were fairly well grown they were moved to the woods, along with one in six of the bantams, to teach them how to live in the wild. Once the poults had learned to roost up trees the broodies would finally be removed (if they could catch them) and the pheasants left to themselves.

The next development was the moveable pen system. With improvements in the quality of food manufactured for young chicks it became possible to enclose them in pens without having to give them access to grass runs where they could forage for themselves. This reduced the inevitable losses to predators encountered in open-field systems, but increased disease problems. The solution to this was to move the pens regularly onto fresh ground, which gave the system its name. Poults were then released into the woods in much the same way as in the earlier system. It was estimated that a good gamekeeper could raise 1,000 chicks, and the larger British estates employed small armies of keepers to provide sufficient birds for the shooting season.

The biggest development in rearing came when technology did away with the need for the broody foster-mother altogether. The demands of the commercial poultry industry led to improvements in the design of mechanical incubators to hatch eggs, combined with brooder units to keep young chicks warm. These led to great increases in the efficiency of rearing; one person could now rear over 5,000 birds a year. Commercial game farms started to appear, providing birds in this way for many shoots and state bodies. The eggs are almost invariably collected from penned pheasant hens, placed into the incubators in large batches and then moved to the brooder houses

Modern rearing systems are based on technology borrowed from the poultry industry. (Hugo Straker)

In Britain, pheasants are typically released into open-topped pens in woodland when they are six weeks old.

after they have hatched and dried. The chicks are then fed on specialised feeds borrowed from the turkey rearing industry and kept completely indoors for their first few weeks. As they grow they are given access to outside runs, both to increase the space available to the growing birds and to start the process of hardening them off for life in the wild. The age at which they are released varies widely from country to country. In Britain they are usually placed in open-topped release pens in woodland when six weeks old. In parts of Europe where goshawks are common this is often delayed until they reach ten or 12 weeks, whilst in some European and American systems they are released very shortly before the shoot itself to maximise the return to the hunters.

The British system of releasing the birds at six weeks old, some three or four months before the shooting season, is based on a number of factors. The absence of large birds of prey means that their main danger is restricted to foxes, which can be controlled by the gamekeepers. Driven shooting also demands that birds have had time to acclimatise to the wild, grow well-developed plumage and fly well over the guns. The intensity of this system also provides enough money to pay for a keeper to look after them in the wild. In North America many birds are released by state organisations to increase the numbers over large areas with numerous mammalian and avian predators, so releases tend to be just before the season. The American system of walked-up shooting also does not require the birds to be as acclimatised to life in the wild as in Britain, and many commercial hunting clubs release birds immediately before the hunt to maximise the return rate.

THE EFFICIENCY OF REARING

The vast majority of the pheasants released each year are intended to increase the number of birds available to the hunters. So how effective are they at providing extra targets for the guns? The answer varies enormously, according to the type of shooting, the system of rearing and the degree of predator control. At one extreme, British driven shoots commonly shoot 40-45 per cent of the birds they release while another 5 per cent are shot in the next year. These areas release and shoot both sexes and the return rates mentioned previously are only the average. Some estates can manage a 70 per cent return, including

Pheasant releases are widely used to increase hunting opportunities, but what are the long-term effects on the population? (Hugo Straker)

hens caught up at the end of the season for their laying pens. In contrast, the system I first studied in southern Ireland, where small numbers of birds were released to provide birds for walked-up shooting, only gave a 10 per cent return. In Ireland the birds were released in the summer on land with little or no predator control. Although both sexes were released, only the cocks were shot. This combination of early releases, predation and selective shooting all led to poor returns.

North America has a mixed history of releases for a variety of different aims. Starting in the latter half of the last century, a variety of birds from European game farms and directly imported from China were released. The Chinese birds did particularly well and within ten years an initial stock of less than 200 birds in the Willamette Valley in Oregon had risen to around 50,000. Fresh imports and wild trapped birds from other successful releases helped spread the birds into other states – Massachusetts, New Jersey, New York and Pennsylvania – where other populations were established before the turn of the century. The greatest successes of pheasant introduction occurred slightly later in the Midwest, between 1900 and 1910, and were organised by state game departments rather than private individuals. These established the pheasant in what was to prove its prime North American range. From there, further stocking spread the bird into a number of other states to produce its current range.

The success of these initial releases were dramatic to say the least. In the mid-1940s one state, South Dakota, was thought to contain between 16 and 30 million wild birds. These numbers may have been dramatic, but hunters still wanted more and many of the state release programmes set up to introduce them were expanded to allow annual releases into areas where the birds were already established. By the late 1940s over a million birds were being released annually in the 32 states with resident populations. By this time over 70 per cent of the money spent by state bodies on all forms of game management was devoted to pheasant release. The emphasis switched to public relations, bolstering populations in areas where they were declining or not thought to be sufficiently abundant, and offsetting the effects of high hunting pressure in certain areas.

In an attempt to increase locally established populations they also tried spring releases of hens which had been kept over winter in pens from the previous year's game farm production. These were intended to increase the breeding stock but studies showed their survival and breeding success to be particularly poor, and they have largely been discontinued.

North American game management is largely funded by the sale of hunting licences. Studies of the return rates of these state-sponsored pheasant releases showed that they were not an effective way of spending the money. The return rates typically ranged between 5 and 50 per cent of the total released, the highest returns (up to 90 per cent in a few cases) coming from releases just prior to the first day of the shooting season. These studies also found that, given the poor survival rate of the reared birds, they were unlikely to lead to further increases in the already established stocks. Consequently, most states abandoned their stocking programmes and either shifted their emphasis to caring for their wild stocks or gave up active pheasant management altogether.

Rearing still continues in certain areas, and some states release birds on public hunting grounds near metropolitan areas to satisfy high demands. There has also been a rise in the number of commercial hunting clubs, where birds can be released and chased to order, paid for by the individual hunter. Nevertheless, rearing in North America has never followed the European system of large-scale releases for driven shooting. It is a fashion that has not caught on except in a few eastern states, partly because of the system of state-owned shooting rights and a different hunting ethic.

WHAT HAPPENS TO RELEASED BIRDS?

Whatever the reason for release, it is worth looking at the fate of the birds to understand what can and cannot be achieved. When birds are put down into an area with uncontrolled predator populations they seem to fade away rapidly, with very little indication of their fate. The story of the group of sportsmen who release a few hundred birds and then see them gradually dwindle away to nothing is told again and again. It is only natural to assume that they have all moved away for the benefit of the neighbours or that they have adapted so well to life in the wild that they hide from visitors, but the truth is less heartening. Naive birds released into an area with normal levels of predators soon fall prey and the predators themselves learn that there are easy pickings to be made. My own first releases in Ireland suffered just this problem. Half of my birds were lost within the first few weeks and 95 per cent

died within a year. After searching for corpses and the numbered plastic tags that I had fitted to my birds I discovered that predation, particularly by foxes, was by far the main cause of loss. This same story recurs again and again in studies of releases, with predators taking the vast majority of the birds within a few days or weeks of the initial release. It might be nice to think that the birds have happily gone to live elsewhere, but experience suggests that a missing bird is a dead bird.

This need not always be the case, however. British driven shoots have perfected pen designs, electric fencing and fox control techniques that can reduce these losses to acceptable levels of 10–20 per cent of the initial release. The large scale of British releases also seems to help. While a release of 100 birds may suffer heavy losses, a release of 1,000 or 10,000 into the same area may swamp the predators and, although predators may be attracted in and more birds may be lost, the *percentage* loss is much lower.

By searching for the corpses of tagged birds I gained my first impression of reared pheasant mortality rates.

The use of release pens can increase the survival prospects of released birds and allows them time to acclimatise to life in the wild.

The way in which the birds are released also seems to play a part. Just tipping the birds out into the countryside seems to produce the worst returns, while the use of well-designed and well-sited release pens can give better, although more expensive, results. It is not just a question of giving them time to learn about their surroundings; they must learn to feed properly and compete with other birds in the area if they are to stand a chance of breeding successfully.

What stands out about reared birds is that, although they can be produced in large numbers, after release they seem to suffer much higher rates of loss than would be the case for wild birds. For whatever reason they are released, be it establishing a new population, supplementing an existing stock or just increasing the numbers to shoot, their poor survival rate is a real problem.

THE BREEDING SUCCESS OF REARED BIRDS

Despite the poor survival rate of released birds the numbers released are often large, so that even if only a small percentage survive to the breeding season, they might still be able to make a significant contribution to production. There is just one catch: this will only happen if reared birds can

Radiotelemetry provides an invaluable tool when it comes to comparing the breeding success of wild and released pheasants.

breed well and do not displace the resident wild breeding population.

Several studies have compared the breeding success of wild and reared birds. Unfortunately they all reach the same conclusion: reared hens are not very good at producing chicks. It is not that they cannot lay eggs; they are just as good as wild birds in that respect, and they even manage to choose the right sort of nest site, which is not bad considering that they were usually hatched in mechanical incubators. The eggs are also of good quality and have the same hatchability as wild ones. So when it comes to choosing a nest and producing a clutch they seem to do well. The problem lies elsewhere.

We already know that reared birds are very vulnerable to predation. This vulnerability continues through the breeding season and, if anything, becomes worse. During our studies of marked birds, we have radiotracked 193 reared hens and 66 wild ones through the breeding season and the differences are clear. If we had started off with 100 of each at the beginning of March, by the time they were sitting on nests at the end of April, we would already be down to 83 reared hens and 94 wild ones. While sitting on the nest both wild and reared hens are particularly vulnerable, and we tend to lose 25 per cent of each group, bringing the survivors down to 62 reared and 70 wild birds. The big difference comes after nesting. In the 20 days after either losing a nest or hatching a brood, we only lose 2 per cent of the wild hens compared to 36 per cent of the reared ones. This brings the number of survivors down to 68 wild, but only 40 reared hens. Of course many then try to produce a second or even third clutch and the gap widens. By the end of the breeding season we are down to 50 wild and only 16 reared hens and the wild birds have produced four times as many chicks.

If this were the only problem it would not be too bad. If reared hens were an addition to the breeding stock then any chicks they produced would be a bonus. Unfortunately it seems as though they may replace some of the wild birds, and the number of chicks fledged by the population as a whole can actually fall.

In the chapter on nesting I described how, in wild pheasant populations, we found a strong link between the density of breeding birds and their individual chances of fledging a brood. To arrive at this conclusion we identified a range of studies, some of which included reared birds, and the populations that included reared birds had consistently lower rates of production than we would have expected given the breeding density. Not only that, the greater the proportion of reared birds the greater the difference. It looks as though rearing dilutes the breeding stock with hens that do not breed well and the population ends up with fewer chicks as a result. The size of the breeding stock is often limited by the quality of the habitat, with wild and reared birds competing for places, so reared birds are not an addition to the residents but a threat. Moreover, when people do release birds they usually want to shoot them, so hunting pressure increases. I cannot tell a wild bird from a reared one in flight, and I doubt whether many hunters can either. The result is that rearing can lead to the wild stock being overshot, leaving few wild hens to enter the breeding season. Taken together, these different factors mean that rearing may actually hinder the wild stock and decrease chick production, and the idea of topping up the breeding stock with released birds may actually backfire.

What happens to the numbers of breeding pheasants and their individual success when birds are released?

A broad look at studies from a wide range of different areas is all very well, but do the conclusions hold true on an individual site? Between 1983 and 1987, we studied a population on a 670 acre block of Knoll Farm in Dorset. This was the area where David Hill carried out his studies and which I followed for my first few years at the Game Conservancy Trust. We collected accurate records of the number of birds released, the number of cocks and hens breeding each spring and the number and size of the broods that they produced. The interesting thing was that, for four of the five years, about 170 birds per 100 acres were released on the farm. However, in 1984 no rearing took place and the 1985 breeding population contained only wild birds, old surviving reared birds, or their offspring from the previous year. So comparing breeding success in 1985 with that in the other four years should indicate what happens in the absence of rearing.

In the four years with rearing the breeding population averaged 16 hens per 100 acres, while in 1985 this fell to only just over 8. The years with rearing averaged 12 territorial and 20 non-territorial cocks, while in 1985 there were also 12 territorial cocks but only four non-territorials per 100 acres. Rearing may therefore increase the breeding density of the hens to some extent and raise the number of non-territorial males, but without affecting the number of territories. As I said in the chapter on territories, the number of territories seems to be limited by the habitat.

The breeding success of the hens also varied. In the four years with rearing only 21 per cent of the hens alive in April went on to produce a brood of chicks, compared with just over 50 per cent in 1985 when there were no juvenile hand-reared hens in the population. The age structure of the population in the autumn showed the same picture: 1.1 young per adult in the rearing years compared to 2.1 in 1985. Even though the spring hen population was at its lowest in 1985, these birds still managed to produce 16 chicks per 100 acres as opposed to only nine in the other four years, when the population included reared birds. So our experience on Knoll Farm confirms what we saw when comparing different studies. Rearing may increase breeding hen density, but the productivity of those hens declines and does not lead to an actual increase in the number of chicks produced; the population is diluted with birds that do not breed effectively.

REARING IN A LEAKING BUCKET

Rearing to bolster a declining or scarce wild stock is often referred to as 'topping up' the population. This is in some ways a very apt term, but also one that can give a misleadingly optimistic idea of its effects. All too often the response to dwindling pheasant stocks is to say that we need to release some birds to bring the population back up to the levels of former years. Once we have more birds around they will breed and we will have even more.

The logic of this argument is a bit faulty, however. It runs something like this. We do not have enough birds. The reason we do not have enough birds is that we do not have enough birds. As a rationale, it leads no where. No where does it break the circle and ask what was limiting the population, or what happened to cause the shortage in the first place. There are many reasons for pheasant declines and I have talked about some of the most important elsewhere. But how do releases really affect pheasant numbers?

The idea of topping up conjures up images of a pheasant population being a bit like water in a bucket, the water being the pheasant stock and the bucket their environment. If the water gets too low then pouring in some new water should raise the level – this is the whole idea behind topping up. The trouble is that it ignores the reasons why the level dropped so low in the first place. The important thing is that the bucket leaks. There is a crack in the side, wide at the top and becoming narrower towards the bottom. There is a continual loss of water, and the fuller the bucket, the faster the water leaks out. Fortunately it rains every now and again – the equivalent of the natural production of chicks increasing the pheasant stock – so the bucket is unlikely ever to be completely empty. But if the water level gets too low it is not because of a fault with the water. Rather than pouring in more water and watching it gush out – the equivalent of releasing birds – the common-sense thing to do is to fix the bucket.

The crack can be thought of as representing all the various things that kill pheasants: predators, disease, hunting, food shortage, habitat loss etc. The worse these problems become, the wider the

*Can the release of birds really help 'top up' a
declining wild pheasant population?*

crack is and the closer it stretches to the bottom
of the bucket. Well-planned management can
help reduce their importance, narrow the crack,
and keep in more water.

Rearing is only good for two things: introducing birds into an area where there are no wild
birds and providing extra targets for hunters. In
terms of helping a dwindling wild stock, it is
probably the worst thing that can be done. Not
only will the poor breeding success of the reared
hens probably depress chick production, but by
concentrating on rearing, effort and resources are
diverted away from tackling the real causes.

WHAT IS WRONG WITH REARED BIRDS?

Looking at the successes and failures of releases
prompts the question, 'Why do reared birds have
such poor survival prospects?', a much easier
question to ask than to answer. I can think of five
main reasons why they may not be able to
perform particularly well, but my list is by no
means exhaustive.

The first reason may be that most pheasants are
reared with no chance to learn from a parent,
even a surrogate mother as was the case when
they were reared under broody chickens. It is
hard to judge just how important this is. As
humans it is impossible for us to imagine being
prepared for life without a parent to teach us the
basics, but the malifowl of south-east Asia, a very
close relative of the pheasant, never sees its
parents and is born with all the behaviour
patterns it needs for later life. These birds lay their
eggs in piles of rotting vegetation which provide
the warmth to incubate them. The chicks hatch,
survive and breed with no assistance from their
parents.

A second reason may be that many reared birds
are produced from captive laying flocks on game
farms or, as is often the case in Britain, from hens
surviving from previous releases which are
caught at the end of the shooting season. Both
methods could be imposing unnatural forms of
selection on the stock, favouring birds with
certain characteristics that may not necessarily be
the best ones for life in the wild. In penned
stocks, selection may be for docile birds that feed
a lot, and therefore survive well in captivity and
lay plenty of eggs. In the case of caught birds on

107

Game-farm pheasant chicks have no contact with their natural parents. (Hugo Straker)

British driven shoots, the intense shooting pressure on the strongest flying birds may only leave those that are poor flyers. For this reason, the Italians and Hungarians maintain purely wild bird areas that are never shot, in order to provide a pristine source of birds for their game farms. It is certainly possible that, over the years, we have selected a strain of pheasants based on something other that their ability to survive and breed in the wild.

Thirdly, hand-reared birds are invariably reared in dense groups. For a bird whose social order is based on relatively small flocks for much of the year, being raised in groups of hundreds or thousands may be a stressful experience, disrupting the natural pecking order that develops in the wild. Some classic studies on rats have found that animals reared in unnaturally large groups ended up as poor breeders, had less efficient immune systems and were easily dominated by others reared in more normal conditions. Reared pheasants may be neurotic when they are released.

Fourthly, the high densities of birds during the

rearing process also make them more prone to disease, as every game farmer knows. The obvious effect of this is a proportion of birds die during the rearing process, which is clearly a problem. More worrying, however, are the possible effects of these infections on the birds' later survival prospects. Even rearing birds in high-quality hygienic conditions may be a problem as they do not then have the chance to build up a natural immunity to cope with the diseases they encounter after release.

Finally, the actual management of the birds after release could be part of the problem. The high numbers released into an area may act as a honeypot for predators, whether or not the birds themselves are naive. Supplementary feeding, which is an important part of the more successful release programmes, may lead to birds that cannot recognise, or cannot properly digest, natural foods.

These five possibilities – lack of parental influence, genetic changes in the stocks, stress, disease and post-release management – are all worth looking at in some detail. A large part of our work at the Game Conservancy Trust has been to try to understand which of these are most important, and, in particular, which can be solved to produce a reared bird with a better chance of surviving and breeding in the wild. It is worth taking a closer look at which of these possibilities may be important and which ones could be changed, at reasonable cost, through management.

PARENTAL INFLUENCE

The influence of a parent on pheasant chick development starts earlier than might be imagined. The incubating hen calls to the chicks while they are still growing in the egg, and the chicks actually call to each other. This seems to be the period when they get to recognise certain calls as warnings or as safety. A group of Americans once played cock pheasant alarm calls to unhatched eggs. When the chicks hatched, they thought that this was the sound of their mother and ran towards it. Normally reared chicks run and hide at the same noise.

Work on grey partridges by Simon Dowell at the Game Conservancy Trust has also shown that chicks all hatch with a hiding response to strange sights or noises. However, the presence of a parent is necessary if they are to learn when it is really necessary to hide. The parent tells the chicks when they have done it right and so they learn what is dangerous and what is not. Partridge chicks reared without a parent start off by reacting to everything and then soon stop and hardly bother to react at all to approaching danger. Anyone who has seen groups of reared pheasants standing aimlessly in the middle of the road will recognise their problems when it comes to recognising danger. The importance of this is hard to determine. Reared pheasants can of course soon learn what is dangerous after release. The first year I reared pheasants, I spent many hours watching their behaviour in the release pen. A sparrowhawk had also found the pen and spent the first few days trying to catch the poults. Luckily the pen was well supplied with shrubs and the poults soon learned to run and hide. To my knowledge I only lost one bird to the hawk. The interesting thing was that, within one day, the released birds had learned that sparrowhawks are to be avoided, despite never having been exposed to one before, and no parent being there to warn them. As soon as the songbirds near the pen started to give alarm calls, before the hawk had even come into sight, the poults would run to the safety of the bushes. I am not suggesting that reared pheasants are wonderfully wary animals that can outwit predators, just that they do learn, and can do so quite quickly when the need arises.

Work on partridges suggests that parental influence can help improve reared bird behaviour, but does not increase their overall survival. (Alexis de la Serre)

Would rearing birds with their natural parents lead to better survival? It is not something we have studied with pheasants, but Simon Dowell's work with grey partridges found that rearing birds in the presence of an adult might give them more appropriate behaviours. When they were released, however, they still died at the same rate as hand-reared birds. Learning behaviours from a parent did not help them survive after release.

The high losses of pheasants immediately after release are almost certainly due, in part, to their lack of experience. But there are cheaper and easier ways of solving this problem than trying to rear them with a parent, a complicated and potentially expensive business. In Britain this is done by employing gamekeepers to control foxes, the main predators around the release sites. In North America it is done by releasing the birds just before the shooting season so that there is no time for predators to take many. Moreover, reared birds do adapt to life in the wild – not completely and maybe not very well, but those that survive the shooting season have developed beyond the most vulnerable stage. Developing techniques to educate large numbers of released birds to recognise predators would be expensive, most would still be shot, and they would still face a whole range of other problems that improving their behaviour may not solve.

THE GENETIC ORIGIN OF REARED BIRDS

When people look at reared pheasants they often refer to them as chickens. So have reared pheasant stocks been domesticated in the same way as their barnyard cousins? Would reverting to some pure, wild strain of pheasant solve all the problems? This is not simply a question of how reared birds may perform; if genetics really is a problem then it could have implications for both reared pheasants and wild populations derived from released birds.

Pheasant populations in the midwestern and eastern parts of America have seriously declined in the last 30 years. There has obviously been considerable debate as to the reasons for these declines and it is certain that there is no single cause. Changing agriculture, the increased use of pesticides, rising predator populations and loss of habitat have all played their part. The big ques-

tion for American game managers is not so much why they have declined, but rather what the best way is to bring them back.

One attractive approach has been to introduce new, hopefully more vigorous, strains to an area. This approach has been actively pursued by Michigan's Wildlife Division. Although the history of pheasant introductions to North America is fairly well documented, the source of the birds was often questionable. Although some shipments of wild Chinese birds were involved, there were also others with a European game farm background. It is possible, so the theory goes, that the mixed origins of these birds and their partially domesticated background reduced their flexibility to changing conditions. I have my doubts about this argument, since the success of the original birds introduced to North America and their spread into so many different states suggests that there cannot have been much wrong with them. Having mixed origins should also have increased their variability and their ability to adapt to changing conditions. But it is possible that there may be a strain of pheasant somewhere that would be better adapted to current conditions than the ones they have at present.

Ever since pheasants began to decline in the 1940s, different states have tried to obtain wild birds from China. With the strained diplomatic relations between the two countries there was little hope until the early 1970s when China again began to open her doors. In 1983, Michigan obtained approval from the Sichuan Foreign Affairs Office to collect wild Chinese pheasant eggs as a gift to promote international relations. Sichaun province lies in southern central China and contains a wide variety of different habitats in its huge area, from sub-tropical rice growing areas to remote mountain ranges. It is also home to Strauch's pheasant, a subspecies of the Chinese ring-neck. Strauch's pheasant or, as it was quickly renamed on its importation into America, the Sichuan, lives in shrubby cover and forested areas where they border onto agricultural land. In Michigan, changes in agriculture since the 1940s have led to areas where marginal farmland has reverted to brush, idle fields and small woodlands. The hope was that the Sichuans might be better adapted to these conditions than the current Michigan ring-necks, and that new blood with Chinese ways might help spread the

Has there been unintentional selection in reared birds, or within captive stocks on game farms, that has led to genetic changes and a bird less able to survive in the wild?

Michigan pheasant range into the more wooded areas. In 1985 a team from Michigan went out to collect eggs and chose an area of marginal farmland as similar as possible to the region of Michigan where they hoped to release them.

They changed the traditional game-farming methods they had used in the past in an attempt to maintain the genetic diversity of the new stock. They then set about releasing the birds into their selected area in the south-east of the state, which had low existing pheasant densities. The Sichuan birds were different from the local ring-necks in a number of ways. Early studies suggested that they nested in more woody cover than the local birds, which boded well for colonising the more wooded areas. However, later studies showed no difference in nest site selection between introduced and local birds. Moreover, their survival after release was, if anything, worse than local ring-necks reared and released in the same way. The hens laid smaller clutches and they were

wilder and jumpier to handle than the typical birds held at the state's game farm. The releases into these areas certainly led to local increases in the pheasant breeding stock, as measured by the numbers of crowing males heard in the spring. However, releasing birds of any sort can lead to temporary increases in the population. The crucial question is will the population remain at a high level once the releases stop? Although no firm conclusions have been released, the fact that they have not been proclaiming their success suggests that the project may not have achieved all that they hoped. The last I heard was that Michigan was scaling down its involvement with Sichuans. So too have many of the other states who initially had such high hopes of increasing their populations with new blood.

The Michigan trial is only the latest attempt to improve pheasant populations by changing the bird rather than the environment. In the 1950s Wisconsin was experimenting with Japanese green pheasants. They hoped that they would lay nests later than the typical ring-necks to avoid being killed in large numbers during hay mowing, and that they would expand the pheasant range into areas with more woody cover, just as the

Michigan project hoped. At about the same time, Ohio tried expanding their pheasant range by releasing a hybrid of five different species, known as the quintex pheasant, selectively bred to show features that were thought to be advantageous. Neither of these attempts is well documented and, in biology, nobody fails to publish details of a project that has been a success. Certainly the quintex pheasant project was abandoned after they were shown to have no advantages over the resident ring-necks.

Nowhere have I come across convincing accounts of the release of a new strain turning a pheasant decline around, despite numerous attempts and millions of dollars spent in North America. Changing the strain of bird is just too attractive an idea. At first sight it does seem to make a great deal of sense. When a new strain is brought into captivity, it usually seems wilder and jumpier than the typical stock, and there are cases where a new strain has colonised an area where previous introductions have failed. But the success of releases into virgin territory is not proof that new strains could do better than the residents

Rufus Sage, seen here with two melanistic hens, followed the survival and breeding success of pheasants from wild and game-farm type strains. (Rufus Sage)

in areas where things have gone well in the past. The fact is that nowhere have the high expectations of reversing declines by releasing new strains been met in terms of real results.

The American Sichuan experience has a number of parallels with work we did near Cambridge in 1991. British estate owners have similar ideas to the Americans when it comes to the quality of their resident birds. There was a commonly held view that introducing new, wild blood might invigorate their stocks. Unlike the Americans, the concern in Britain was not so much the decline in wild birds, but the fact that the released birds on which so much of British pheasant shooting relies were seen to be getting bigger and fatter, and becoming slower and lower targets for the guns on driven shooting days. Rather than importing Chinese birds, British attempts to increase the genetic quality of the stock have relied on birds from well-established, historically wild populations in the treeless fenlands of East Anglia or birds imported from Scandinavia or North America. These are all regions with some areas where little or no releasing has occurred for many decades.

The birds from these areas are smaller than the typical game-farm stock, often by 20–30 per cent, and many of the features noted in Sichuan birds in Michigan are also apparent: smaller clutches among the females, more difficulties when rearing them in pens and an increased wildness and wariness.

Doug Wise, a Cambridgeshire man with a long interest in pheasant shooting and involvement with our own work at the Game Conservancy Trust, proposed that we should monitor a rearing programme he was involved with. He was collecting hens and eggs from verified wild pheasant areas in the east of England with the intention of releasing their offspring on a nearby shoot. Doug was particularly interested to see how the flying ability of these birds compared with normal game-farm birds and whether their use could improve the long-term production of the breeding population. This seemed too good an opportunity to miss, so we started a joint project to follow these birds and a comparable group from the Game Conservancy Trust's own game-farm stock. We monitored them from release and through the hunting season to the next round of breeding in the summer.

We compared the survival and breeding success of different pheasant strains, reared and released in the same way but derived from game-farm and wild type strains.

In 1990, Doug raised almost 1,000 chicks of each group under identical conditions, and they were tagged and released that summer, mixed together in a number of release pens on Kingston Wood Farm near Cambridge. We really got involved in monitoring them once the shooting season started. The second thing we were interested in was whether the wild-type birds bred better than the typical game-farm stock. Rufus Sage, who had just completed a masters degree looking at insect availability in Scottish pine forests as food for capercaillie chicks, came down to Cambridge and we started a study to follow hens of both groups through the breeding season.

Rufus caught 50 hens, 25 of each type, in early spring and fitted them with small radiotransmitters. For the next few months he drove round and round the farm chasing the bleeps to keep track of each bird's performance. Would a strain of birds more recently brought in from the wild have more natural canniness and be better able to survive and rear a brood of chicks? We did find some differences – the wild type tended to lay fewer eggs and nested in more open areas than the game-farm birds – but frustratingly, there was really very little difference in their breeding success. Both the wild and game-farm strains did poorly, as is typical of released birds. From this study and some of the work with Sichuans in Michigan therefore there is no clear evidence to suggest that releasing a wild strain of reared birds has any benefit in terms of breeding success. They may seem wilder in the pens, they are usually a bit smaller, they may fly a bit better and they lay fewer eggs, but they do not seem to breed any better or rear more chicks. Interestingly, the Michigan birds were brought in from a wooded part of China and tended to nest in the woods more often than the local birds, while the wild-type we were dealing with in Cambridge came from open, treeless fen country and nested in the open more often than the game-farm strain. So it may be that the behaviours that tell a hen where to nest are inherited and vary from strain to strain. I cannot be sure, and it may not be important, but it is interesting, for a pheasant biologist at least.

The evidence for the poor performance of reared birds being due to genetics looks slim. The absence of studies showing differences in survival or breeding success when different strains are released is certainly not due to a lack of trying.

Huge amounts of money have been spent on this over the years. Moreover, if the problem with reared birds really was genetic we would also expect their poor performance to be passed on to their offspring, but in practice, this does not seem to happen. Most of the wild birds in our own studies have probably been the offspring of surviving reared birds, yet they survive and breed well. It would be wonderful if genetics really were at the root of the problem, as it would be such an easy thing to fix, but all the evidence is against it and we will have to look elsewhere.

DISEASE AND PARASITES

When I started work on pheasants I had the view that if diseases did not kill the birds outright then they were not a problem, or were only a reflection of the bird being under stress for some other reason. From about 450 birds that I released in Ireland, I found 50 dead within the pen from disease. I was not a particularly good pheasant rearer and I never found a bird outside the pen that had died from disease, so I concluded that disease was only important when the birds were in the pens. It is all to easy to apply human experience to animals and come up with the wrong answer. If we develop a disease we become sick and then, with a bit of luck, we recover. With pheasants and many other animals, it is a different story. Many parasites and diseases are with them for much of their lives and are a constant drain on their resources. The diseases rarely even kill them outside of release pens. Any bird whose performance is reduced is usually taken by a predator before it can become obviously sick or incapacitated. It is a bit like saying that a bad cold does not kill you. This is true if you can just go to bed and sleep it off, but imagine what it would do if you had to search for your own food in a forest full of tigers! Looked at in this light, my conclusions were all wrong. Rather than the deaths through disease which occur in release pens showing that this is the only place where disease occurs, I think it is fairer to say that release pens are the only places where the birds are protected enough from predators not to be eaten once disease begins to take hold. Sick birds do not die of disease, they die of predation.

What first brought home to me the potential of

If the poor performance of reared hens were due to genetics, we would expect their shortcomings to be passed on to their chicks.

parasites and disease in what appear to be healthy animals was Peter Hudson's work on red grouse. He had been catching hens in the spring and giving them drugs to rid them of parasites, with dramatic effects on their survival and reproduction. It looked as though ridding the birds of parasites improved their condition, raised their breeding success and made them less likely to fall prey to predators. Reared pheasants are host to a whole range of parasites and the conditions in which they live could make them particularly vulnerable to infection. We therefore decided that parasites deserved a closer look.

First we collected a range of birds from local estates at the end of their day's shooting and examined the parasites in their guts. It would have been good to have been able to look at microscopic blood parasites, viruses and so on as well, but cost limited us to the relatively large and easy to find worms. One worm looked particularly interesting – *Heterakis,* which lives in the ceacae, or blind gut, the pheasant's equivalent of

our appendix. We found that almost all the birds were carrying some of these worms, that the numbers we were finding in these reared birds were much higher than anything recorded from wild pheasant populations and that birds with high levels of infection tended to have less fat, and were not in as good condition.

Simply knowing which worms were present does not, of course prove that they are a problem. Even the discovery that birds with lots of worms were thinner could be interpreted in two ways: either the birds were thin because they had worms, or they had worms because they were already thin for some other reason and were open to infection. We therefore decided to repeat Peter Hudson's work on grouse and catch some pheasants for dosing in the spring. Maureen Woodburn, who had been with our project since the beginning, was particularly keen on this work and took it on as part of a PhD, dosing and monitoring the birds through the breeding season. We ended up with three categories of birds to study: two different groups of reared birds, one of which was given a drug to remove the worms while the other was just given water, and a group of wild birds on the same areas that was also only given water. Maureen fitted 30 birds of each group with radiotransmitters and followed their survival and breeding success through the spring and summer.

The results were really quite dramatic. From what we knew about the comparative success of wild and reared hens, we expected to find a difference. Sure enough, the wild birds had much better survival and breeding success than the undosed reared group. One hundred wild hens alive in March went on to produce 57 nests and hatch 180 chicks. For the undosed reared hens the figures were 30 nests and only 25 chicks hatched per 100 hens. The interesting bit was how the dosed reared birds compared. They actually came out very similarly to the wild group, one hundred of them producing 55 nests and 220 chicks hatched. By dosing the reared hens in spring it looked as though we could improve their survival and breeding success to a level similar to the wild stock on the same area.

of the dosed reared birds and 39 per cent of the undosed birds per month during the breeding season. However, when we looked just at the time they were actually sitting on the nest, we were losing 58 per cent of the wild hens, 54 per cent of the undosed reared group but only 27 per cent of the dosed group per month. As we had found before, it looked as though both wild and reared hens were equally vulnerable to predation when they were on the nest. The interesting thing was that the dosed reared group had much better survival during nesting than either the wild or normally reared hens.

Dosing a hen pheasant to remove parasitic worms in her gut. (Maureen Woodburn)

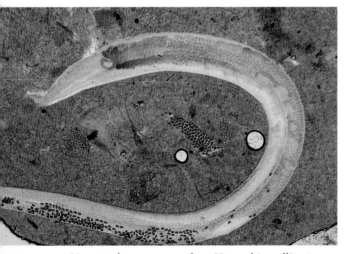

Nematode worms, such as Heterakis gallinarum, *may reduce the body condition of heavily infected birds.* (Maureen Woodburn)

This was not to say that we had produced a reared hen that was exactly the same as a wild one, or that the wild birds might not also have benefited from being dosed, something we didn't look at. It did suggest that parasites were a real problem when it came to hen pheasant survival and breeding success in this particular population. Looking in more detail at the survival of the three groups also showed some interesting differences. Excluding time spent on the nest, we were losing 12 per cent of the wild birds, 23 per cent

There is a lot more work needed before we can really say what was happening, but Peter Hudson's work with grouse also found that dosing hens made them less likely to be lost to predators. His studies of grouse used pointing dogs to locate birds on the nest by scent. He found that his dogs had a great deal of problem finding dosed hens compared to undosed ones. Possibly the worms interfere with the control of scent by the hen. They certainly cause part of her gut to become swollen and this may make her smell more when on the nest. It is hard to be sure but it could be that wormy birds pass wind more often and less controllably than dosed hens, making it easier for predators to smell them on the nest!

From Maureen's study it was clear that removing worms helped the reared hens. However, we know that her birds had quite high levels of worms to start with. Whether her results would have been as dramatic on an area with lower worm numbers remains uncertain, and we need to know more about why there were so many worms in the first place. None the less, Maureen's work is the first to show that it is possible to help reared birds breed more effectively. What we need now are large-scale trials, putting out dosed food for hens over large areas and seeing how performance changes compared to other populations.

FEEDING

Of all the management methods used to help the birds after release, feeding is one of the most important. From the time when they are first put into the release pen until the end of the shooting season, reared pheasants on British driven shoots are provided with food, usually wheat. This is very sensible and produces healthy, fit birds, and I am sure it improves their chances of survival. Certainly, keepers who do not feed their birds well tend to get lower return rates. But one problem that could arise is what happens at the end of the shooting season when this unlimited food supply is cut off. All of a sudden birds which have never had to forage for themselves are faced with having to scrape an unfamiliar living from natural food sources, and at the time of year when this food is most scarce. To make matters worse this is the very time when their energy demands are starting to increase in preparation for the breeding season.

The idea that food shortage may be a problem for reared birds has long interested me. Since I first started radiotracking pheasants in Ireland I have come across thin hens during the breeding season – never often enough to get a real idea of

In 1994 and 1995 we increased the spring food available to released birds by using small hoppers to see if we could improve their body condition and breeding success.

what is happening, but enough to make me think that reared birds are losing too much weight to be healthy. Of course, most birds lose weight while on the nest, but when I came across hens that were so thin that they could hardly walk, let alone fly, it made me think that there might be more to it. Finding funds has always been a problem and it took me ten years before I could finally get sponsorship to look at just how much weight reared hens may be losing, and whether giving them more food might help.

In 1993 Andrew Christie-Miller, the owner of Clarendon Park where we do much of our work, introduced us to an agricultural supply company, SCATS. They were willing to support our work and in 1994 we set up an experiment to look at this problem in more detail. Andrew Hoodless and Roger Draycott started work on what proved to be a most interesting study.

In Britain most reared birds are fed with wheat, either from hoppers or spread daily on woodland rides. At the end of the shooting season in February, and after a brief period when the keepers catch stock for their laying pens, this feeding usually stops. Even where it does not, any feeding that does go on tends to be in the middle of the woods, where few birds will make use of it, since most of them are off looking for suitable breeding sites at the woodland edge. What we wanted to do was put feed hoppers where the birds were most likely to use them, in the cock's territories, and to see if this helped.

Clarendon Park covers some 5,000 acres and we chose six 250 acre blocks to include in our experiment. In three of them we just left the birds to their own devices, and once the food in the keeper's hoppers had run out in March the birds had to forage for themselves. In the other three areas we put out small five gallon drums full of wheat, strategically placed so that each cock territory contained one or two of them. This basically meant putting one hopper every 50 yards of woodland edge, a total of 50 per 250 acre block. We then radiotagged about 20 released hens in each of the six areas and followed them to see what happened. We also switched the areas during the second year to make sure our results were not just an effect of the particular sites.

We also looked at the diet of both the fed and the unfed groups throughout the spring, collecting droppings by walking up and down fields in each of the squares. Studies of healthy wild pheasant populations show that, in the spring, over 80 per cent of their diet consists of seeds or waste grain, most of the remainder being insects or the growing tips of grasses or various crops. On the unfed squares where the reared birds had to forage for themselves, their diet was almost entirely green matter. Just over 90 per cent was leaves picked from the crops, a very poor-quality diet for a bird that is trying to put on fat for the breeding season, while seeds and waste grain made up only 2 per cent. Where we put out wheat we found that the birds soon made this an important part of their ration, and grain constituted about 50 per cent of the content of their droppings while the proportion of leaf dropped accordingly. Given the chance, the birds gained most of their food from the wheat, unlike the unfed birds, which had to rely on green matter. Studies of captive hen pheasants and chickens in spring suggest that the birds need a diet with an energy content of around 11–12Mj/kg (a measure of the energy per unit weight in the diet) if they are to thrive. Wheat provides 12.2Mj/kg, while grass shoots give only 5.8Mj/kg, so clearly the birds feeding mainly on growing shoots were on a very poor diet indeed.

Apart from just radiotracking birds and collecting droppings, we also collected a sample of hens in February and another in April to see how their body condition had changed. In February, before we started our feeding trial, the hens on both fed and unfed areas had about 80g of fat, the energy reserve that they would burn up during the breeding season. By the end of April, the period when the birds should have been putting on weight as fast as possible, the unfed birds had lost over half of their fat reserves while the fed ones had managed to keep their fat levels constant. Although the fed and unfed birds both started with the same level of fat reserves in February, by April there was a 50g difference between the groups. This was not just a question of the amount of fat, although this was of central importance. By April the unfed birds had lost 15 per cent of their body weight while the fed ones had got slightly heavier. Why unfed reared birds should be losing so much weight during the spring remains to be seen. It could be that they were unfamiliar with a diet that does not come out of a hopper or that a prolonged diet of wheat

How well do reared pheasants adapt to a natural diet once supplementary feeding ceases? (Hugo Straker)

has given them a gut poorly adapted to a natural diet. It could also be that other problems, such as high levels of parasites, are such a drain that they cannot sustain their reserves without help; or even that the natural food to be found in modern farmed landscapes is just not good enough. Even if the birds wanted to feed on seeds or waste grain, it is hard to see where they could find a supply in a modern British agricultural landscape. Winter ploughing has meant that few stubble fields are left over the winter and modern harvesters are so efficient that very little grain is wasted. Only time will tell us which of these factors is the cause.

How did these differences actually affect the birds? First, it looked as though the hoppers led to greater densities of birds settling to breed in the fed areas. We had counted the number of breeding birds at Clarendon for a number of years prior to this study and it seemed as though the hoppers led to about a 50 per cent increase in the numbers that remained to breed. We could not prove that we had increased the overall breeding density on the estate, just that we had convinced more birds to stay in the fed areas to breed. Quite how improving the food supply might affect breeding densities over large areas remains an interesting question. It is possible that by reducing the need for spring dispersal we

As part of our feeding experiment we collected pheasant droppings from fed and unfed areas to compare the foods they were eating.

might actually raise survival rates and the size of the breeding stock, but this needs larger-scale trials than the one at Clarendon. Increasing the number of territories in an area by feeding also tells us that food is something that determines how many there normally are. In the chapter on territories I described how woodland edges next to arable crops held more territories than those near grassland, and how this might reflect the quality of the food they provide. Our feeding experiments confirm this. Food availability and the quality of the woodland edges work together to determine the number of available territories.

The important part of the experiment was to discover how well the hens actually bred. We did not find any great differences in the dates when fed and unfed birds started nesting, or the number or hatchability of the eggs they laid into the nests. It therefore appears that, however undernourished they are, hens will sacrifice their own body condition to produce a good clutch of eggs. There was also no difference in nest success. What did come through was that the hens in the fed squares initiated more nests because of their rather better survival rate and the greater chance of going on to lay a second or third clutch if the first one failed. Consequently, hens on the fed squares produced 60 per cent more nests and hatched 40 per cent more chicks than their unfed counterparts.

So what does this study tell us about reared birds? By improving their diet we were able to increase the number of nests and hatched chicks, but was the problem in the unfed areas due to the reared birds or was it a reflection of the habitat? At the moment it is hard to tell. Certainly the increase in rearing that has occurred on many British estates has been partly a response to declines in their wild pheasant populations. We should therefore not expect the habitat to be ideal for the birds, otherwise the wild stock would not have declined in the first place. We really need to know how wild birds would have fared on the same area to draw any firm conclusions. The point, however, is that the breeding success of reared birds in this area could be improved through the use of a relatively simple management technique.

CAN WE SOLVE THE PROBLEMS OF REARING?

Many of the shortcomings of rearing can be attributed to a lack of understanding of what releases can and cannot do. They can establish pheasant populations in new areas, they can lead to short-term increases in numbers to improve the hunting, but they do not lead to long-term increases in pheasant stocks; as we have seen, if anything they may suppress the productivity of the resident breeding population.

Understanding the limitations of releases is important, but people still want to rear birds to maintain the shooting while also starting to manage the environment to help the wild birds. The problem is that the poor breeding success of released hens may mean that improving wild bird management can be an uphill struggle.

A short-term solution to the problem of the poor breeding success of reared hens has been to do away with them altogether. If a shoot wants a combination of reliable numbers of birds and the benefits of wild production then one alternative has been cock-only management. The idea behind this is that if only males are released and the hunting is restricted to them then, given time and the right sort of management, the female population should become completely wild. This assumes that the problems with released bird breeding success have nothing to do with genetics, and this is probably the case. Under a cock-only regime it does not matter what sort of male fertilises the hens as long as the hens themselves have been hatched and reared by a natural parent, with all the skills, experiences and behaviours that this seems to entail.

As a system it does seem to have a number of advantages. Apart from anything else, releasing cocks only on British shooting estates tends to give a higher return rate of birds released to birds shot: around 60 per cent as opposed to 40-50 per cent when both sexes are released together, possibly because cocks are less inclined to wander away from the release pen. It also allows a population of wild and productive hens to be established side by side with a reared pheasant shoot. It certainly seems to work, although we have never followed an estate right through from starting cock-only releases to the establishment of a viable wild shoot. I have, however, counted breeding stocks on estates that have been trying cock-only releases for a number of years. One in particular, where this releasing system had been combined with habitat management and predator control, held the highest density of wild hens that I have seen in Britain, over 40 per 100 acres, and they were just as productive as would be expected from a wild population. On this area they seemed to be able to get the benefits of a wild stock together with the security of a reared one.

Cock-only releasing also has its problems, however, and in terms of a long-term solution, I think they are quite serious. First it appears artificial, which makes it unacceptable to many hunters, particularly those whose eyesight is not as good as it used to be, when it comes to restricting themselves to shooting only males on a day's hunt. It also upsets many game farmers who are faced with requests for only male chicks and are left with with the excess females. This is not a major problem if only a few of their customers want to follow this system, as they can always increase the proportion of females they give to their other clients, but it could be a difficulty in the future. If the only people going in for this system were those looking for a short-term stop-gap to ensure that they could continue shooting reasonable numbers of birds while allowing a wild population to re-establish itself after years of releasing, this would be fairly unimportant. The problem is that the higher return rates make it attractive for those interested in increasing their returns. As a long-term policy I can see it leading to a split between game farmer and hunters while also making pheasant rearing even harder to justify to the general public.

The whole idea of releasing birds to increase the shooting also has a dubious political future. In many people's eyes it seems cruel to rear and nurture a bird simply to then try to shoot it, although I think reared pheasants have a much better life than the broiler chickens that so many of us are happy to eat. Many people, of course,

Releasing pheasants can be an effective way of increasing the hunting opportunities, but may depress the productivity of the population. (Hugo Straker)

are also against the whole idea of shooting for sport, and rearing is an easy target for them to criticise. As a consequence, rearing has been banned in the Netherlands and is under intense scrutiny in a range of other European countries. But it is all too easy to criticise rearing without understanding its effects. If it is held up as a way of supporting or supplementing the wild stocks, then it is currently doomed to failure. However, if it can be shown to encourage landowners and hunters to invest in the management of the countryside, to the benefit of a wide range of other species, then I believe it can have a future if carried out responsibly.

What is really needed is a better understanding of why reared hens, once they have survived the shooting season, seem to be at such a disadvantage when it comes to producing chicks and whether there are ways of improving their performance. My gut feeling is that a system of improving the nutritional status of released hens in the spring holds out the best hope. This could be by supplementary feeding, improving the wild food available to the hens or removing their parasites, or best of all a combination of all three. Beyond this, the survival prospects of the chicks must also be increased. The pointers are there, but we need to try out various strategies to see what actually works. If we can uncover the reasons for the poor survival rates and find a solution, then we may be on the road to having the best of both worlds – not just the benefits of predictable hunting from releases, but also the satisfaction of helping our wild stocks at the same time.

Walked-up shooting was the original form of pheasant hunting in Britain and is still widely practised internationally, particularly in America. (Hugo Straker)

SHOOTING

The pheasant's success has been due to its value to man, and this value revolves around shooting. Accurate figures are hard to come by, and may not even exist, but probably something like 50 million pheasants are shot each year. Of these, 10 million or so are killed annually in North America, 30–40 million in Europe – a large proportion of which are released birds – and a few million elsewhere. The methods of hunting also vary enormously between different regions, but they basically fall into three broad categories: subsistence hunting, walked-up shooting and driven shooting.

Pheasants have long been a prized food item and in many parts of China they are still caught and eaten whenever the opportunity arises. They are not protected under Chinese law and can be hunted all year round, except in nature reserves and national parks. Snares, guns, hawks and traps all play their part and hunting of this sort goes on in all seasons. Hunting is done mainly for food although some shot birds are sold and others are killed for crop protection – farmers complain that the pheasants are an important crop pest in some areas and they will sometimes use poisoned baits to reduce their numbers.

Shooting for sport is rare in China but it is the main method of pheasant hunting in most of the rest of their range. Pheasants were introduced to Europe and North America largely for their sporting value. Although falcons and other birds of prey have long been used for hunting game, modern methods of hunting really began with the invention of firearms. The first guns date from 1338 and by the 1480s weapons firing single lead projectiles were being used to kill deer. Initially pheasants and other gamebirds were shot on the ground, but during the 1560s it became both possible and fashionable to shoot birds in flight. This practice reached Britain in the 1680s and soon became accepted as the only 'sporting' way to kill a bird. By the early part of the nineteenth century a conventional day's shooting might involve a small group of three or four sportsmen using pointing dogs to locate the birds and then flush them for the kill.

The single-barrelled, muzzle-loading weapons in use in the early nineteenth century were slow to reload and unreliable, but the middle of the century saw the development of a prototype percussion lock and the advent of breech-loading guns in 1847. Sportsmen now had a reliable, light firearm capable of rapid shooting and the basic design of the modern shotgun has remained largely unchanged since.

In Europe, where the ownership of land was long the preserve of the aristocracy, the right to hunt game was usually restricted to the nobility. Charles II of England only allowed the richest 5 per cent of landowners to hunt game, even on their own land, and the penalties for breaking the hunting regulations were particularly severe. In the 1750s the penalty for poaching a rabbit was three months' imprisonment or a £5 fine, equivalent to half a year's wages for the average farm labourer. For a deer this rose to £30 or a year in jail, while the owner of the poached deer could demand transportation or death if the animal had been taken from within his park. By the time modern firearms became widespread, these punitive laws had been revoked, but although the right to hunt was more widely enjoyed, the costs of shooting rose so that formal driven shooting was beyond the means of any but the very rich.

The rise of driven shooting in the late nineteenth century depended on three factors: the perfection of the modern shotgun, the expansion of the railways which brought the countryside within easy access of London and its society, and the lead given by Queen Victoria's son the Prince of Wales, later to become King Edward VII. From being the pastime of small groups of hunters, game shooting in Britain underwent a revolution. To compete in the social circles of the Prince's court it was necessary to provide huge numbers of birds to satisfy the demand. No expense was spared and the costs of driven shooting bankrupted a number of large landed families. A saying at the time reflected the economics of pheasant shooting: 'Up gets a guinea, bang goes a penny-halfpenny, and down comes half a crown.' The costs were high, but the scale was also large. King George V and his son, later King Edward VIII, shot at Hall Barn with Lord Burnham in 1913 when the British record of 3,937 pheasants were shot. The King later said, 'Perhaps we overdid it today.' (Count Karolyi's guests at Tot Magyar in Hungary hold the world record at 6,125 in 1909.) Shooting on this scale could become a full-time occupation. The second Marquess of Ripon amassed a lifetime kill of 556,813 between 1867 and 1923, including nearly a quarter of a million pheasants and half that number of partridges.

The system that led to these huge numbers was the driven shoot, or battue. Rather than the hunters walking up to the birds and shooting at them as they flew away, driven shooting relied on a team of beaters pushing the birds towards a line of stationary guns, who would then shoot at the birds as they flew towards them. From a situation where the number of birds shot depended on how far the guns were willing to walk, the size of the bag now depended on the efficiency of the beaters and the skill of the gamekeeper in maintaining high densities on the land. Lord Leicester of Holkham Hall in Norfolk first perfected the technique. Using teams of beaters and walking guns they gradually pushed huge numbers of birds from his estate into one wood, the famous Scarborough Clump. The guns then lined up three deep at one end and the birds were pushed out to them. A single drive of this wood in 1898 took all day and accounted for 760 pheasants.

As the demand for this form of shooting increased, the emphasis was on high densities of birds. This allowed a number of different drives in a day, each containing a large number of birds. Intensive habitat management and predator control were necessary to produce these densities, while many estates relied on rearing to supplement their wild stocks. At the turn of the century there was hardly a part of rural Norfolk that was not patrolled by a gamekeeper, and 20,000 birds were being released annually on the Prince of Wales's estate at Sandringham.

The First World War saw the decline of these great estates. The finances once used to kill pheasants were put to more deadly use and the power of the landed aristocracy went into decline. The number of gamekeepers in Britain, which had risen from 15,000 in 1871 to 23,000 just before the war, fell back to 13,000 by 1921 and to only 5,000 after the Second World War. However, driven shooting remains the normal method of pheasant hunting and, with improvements in the technology of pheasant rearing, it is now a much cheaper proposition. The great estates and the huge bags enjoyed by the Edwardian have gone; but there are now more pheasants shot in Britain than at the turn of the century, albeit on a much larger number of smaller shoots. Driven pheasant shooting, although still an expensive sport, is no longer the sole domain of the super-rich.

In Britain the right to shoot game lies with the landowner, and the open season during which the birds can be shot is long. For pheasants it runs from the beginning of October to 1 February. There are no limits to the number that can be killed per day, or any restrictions on killing hens. The responsibility for limiting the harvest lies with the landowner. This is in complete contrast to the situation in North America, where the game are considered to be held in trust by the state, and the harvest is closely controlled by public agencies.

It has been said that the pheasant is a typical American citizen, 'a blend of Old World races and origins, alloyed in the New World's melting pot and tempered for survival in a new environment'. The bird has followed man, and in particular the strong. Starting in the ancient civilisations of China it conquered Europe with the Romans and reached its peak there in the days of empire at the end of the last century. The twentieth century has been described as the American century, and pheasants there have shared in this success.

In much of the United States the pheasant shooting season is short by European standards, typically three weeks long and starting in October. A hunter must first buy a licence from a hunting goods store or a state game agency, although the regulations vary between states. This licence usually grants permission to kill two cock pheasants per day throughout the season, although few hunters reach this limit. Most only go out for three or four days' pheasant shooting per year. The majority of the birds are therefore shot on the opening day of the season or at the weekends. The shot game cannot then be sold or bartered, although it may be given away. The system is designed to spread the harvest among as many people as possible and to discourage commercial hunters who might wish to profit from the sale of meat. As the game is held in trust by the state there is little direct incentive for landowners to provide suitable habitat or otherwise manage their farms to produce more birds. This contrasts with the situation in Britain, where the sale of shooting can often be a significant source of income for a farm and it is in the owner's interest to provide habitat for the birds. There are areas where the right to shoot can be sold, and in a few places this can bring the farmer a profit, but rarely from pheasant shooting – turkeys and bobwhite quail are the species which are usually involved.

The vast majority of pheasants shot in North America are wild birds, but there are states where rearing is common. For instance, in Pennsylvania the State Game Commission releases birds on state game lands or areas belonging to co-operative farmers to increase the opportunities on heavily shot land. These birds are released a week or less before the beginning of the season and further releases may take place during the season itself. In most areas only the cocks are released. However, if the habitat is deemed unsuitable for wild pheasants then both sexes may be released and shot, as happens in some of the more heavily wooded parts of Pennsylvania.

The state game lands in Pennsylvania form a significant part of the total land area – over a million acres in total. The public have the right to hunt over the whole area, provided they have bought a licence. The licence fees are used to fund the management of these lands and the State Game Commission itself. Although the state lands are often sharecropped by farmers, they are also managed to increase the diversity of wildlife, and food crops and cover plots are provided for the birds. There is also a formal programme to encourage private farmers to open up their lands for public hunting. In particular, the state agrees to cover any insurance claims by hunters for injury while hunting on the land, often a worry for farmers. They can also receive assistance from the state in drawing up habitat management plans.

The proportion of the autumn population that is shot is very variable. In North America, where in most states and provinces only the cocks can legally be shot, hunting can take between 50 and 90 per cent of the cock pheasant population, 65–80 per cent being fairly typical. On top of this an illegal kill of 15–20 per cent of the hens is not uncommon, either through mistakes, frustration or a complete disregard for the law. In Britain both sexes can be shot and the level of hunting is usually set by the landowner. On wild pheasant areas in Britain in a reasonable year, managers might aim for a 70 per cent kill of the males and 20–25 per cent of the hens, quite similar to the North American figures. In poor years, they would be more careful with the hens to conserve a larger stock for the next breeding season. Where birds are reared the system is very different. There is much less difference in shooting pressure between the sexes and less concern to conserve the breeding stocks. Between 70 and 90 per cent of the autumn stock of both sexes may be shot although this varies considerably between different shoots.

A BRITISH DRIVEN SHOOT

How is shooting organised on a driven shoot? Clarendon Park is a 5,000 acre estate on the edge of Salisbury in Wiltshire. It is owned by Andrew Christie-Miller and contains a mixture of arable and dairy farming together with over 1,000 acres of forestry, which is concentrated in the centre of the estate. The land is on rolling chalk and the smaller woods and coverts have largely been laid out with shooting in mind. The estate employs three gamekeepers who rear, feed and protect the pheasants from predators. Roy Perks, the head keeper started working on the estate in the 1960s. At that time wild pheasants were still abundant and formed a large part of the annual bag, supplemented by the release of some 2,000 reared birds per year. In common with most farms in this part of the world, the wild game has declined in the face of modern agriculture and the estate has come to rely increasingly on reared birds to maintain, and in fact greatly increase the shooting.

The keepers rear their own birds; in the past they relied on collecting eggs from wild nests and raising them under broody chickens in small coops, a labour-intensive system that has now largely disappeared. Nowadays the estate relies on catching hens at the end of the season, keeping them in pens during the laying season and collecting their eggs to place in mechanical incubators adapted from the poultry industry. The birds are reared indoors for their first few weeks and then allowed access to covered runs to start the process of hardening them off, ready for

release into the wild. At six weeks they are taken out of the rearing unit and placed into large open-topped pens in the woods, a continual process from mid-June until August as different batches of birds are placed into separate pens. The birds have the outermost feathers on one wing clipped when they are put into the pens. This restricts their flight for a couple of weeks until they regrow and keeps them inside the pens until they become fully acclimatised. The pens are placed in sheltered areas of woodland, well provided with open sunning areas and roosting cover. The birds are fed daily by the keepers and, as they mature, are enticed away from the pens to feed, returning each night to roost. This is a critical aspect of running an effective pheasant shoot where reared birds are involved. As the birds establish a set routine, their movements and reactions to being flushed can be predicted with some certainty.

Although the pheasant season starts at the beginning of October, the first day's shooting is usually delayed until towards the end of the month, giving time for the birds to become fully feathered and for the leaves to fall from the trees. The estate operates a mixture of private and let

Many British driven shoots now rely on reared birds to ensure sufficient numbers for shooting.

Many driven shoots use a game-cart to collect birds at the end of each drive.

days. A proportion of the shooting is sold to help cover the costs of the rearing process and the gamekeepers' wages, while the remaining days are for the benefit of the owner and his friends.

The organisation of a driven pheasant shoot is no mean achievement. A typical day involves eight hunters, sometimes accompanied by their own gamekeepers to assist in the loading of the guns, a team of around 20 beaters under the supervision of the estate's keepers, two or three 'pickers-up' with their dogs, who stand behind the line of guns to mark birds as they fall, and a game-cart. These different groups have to be co-ordinated as they travel around the estate to seven or eight different drives in a day. The beaters enter a wood at one end, and the guns and pickers-up line up at the other, with the game-cart waiting to move in at the end of the drive.

The ideal on a driven pheasant shoot is to provide high, fast birds that will be testing targets for the guns. It is also important to ensure that all the guns get some shooting on all the drives and that the birds flush in small groups rather than in one big rush. The layout and planning of the drive is therefore of paramount importance and

is something of an art. The keeper must be able to predict where the birds are going to flush from and where they will fly to, and then arrange the guns in the best position. This is where the siting of release pens and feeding sites is of particular importance. When pheasants are flushed they will often tend to try to head for somewhere they feel secure, often the roost site or release pen in the case of reared birds. The basic principle is therefore to feed them out into an area away from the pen and then drive them back home towards it. But this is a gross oversimplification of the work involved. Debating different ways in which a particular piece of cover could be driven, or the precise siting of a new wood, can fill many hours and no two people will ever come up with the same answer.

A day's driven pheasant shooting typically starts with the hunters, or guns as they are called, and beaters meeting at 8.30 or 9 o'clock. They then move off to the first drive. The beaters on Clarendon travel in a trailer behind a tractor and the guns follow later in an assortment of four-wheel drive vehicles. The guns line out at the end of a wood or game crop, their positions marked by posts or pegs arranged beforehand by the keepers. These are placed about 40 yards apart so that each has a good chance of some shooting, and so that they are sufficiently separated not to shoot at each other's birds. The position each gun will take at each drive is determined by lot at the start of the day and the guns rotate through a set series of positions so that each has a chance to be in the best position on at least one drive. The wait while the beaters work through the woods can be long, so most come well prepared for the English winter weather. Waterproof jackets, thick tweed trousers that reach to the knees, heavy woollen socks, a flat cap and rubber boots are the standard dress.

Meanwhile the beaters line up at the opposite end of the cover and walk slowly towards the guns, tapping sticks as they come in order to push the birds in front of them. The beaters must keep in line as they advance to stop birds cutting back

The British weather requires well-planned clothing for a day in the field.

and they must also ensure that the birds are not flushed so early that they do not fly over the line. As the birds reach the end of the cover there is often a piece of string covered in plastic strips or sewelling hung across their path and gently shaken by a beater. This stops them running to the end of the wood and, as the other beaters approach, ensures that the birds flush while still inside the cover rather than at its edge. Controlling the flush of the birds is one of the most critical parts of a pheasant drive. The beaters must only push gently to create small flushes while the sewelling or other flushing point must be placed so that the birds are already at treetop height as they leave the cover and come into sight of the guns. On a successful drive the beaters will then produce a steady flow of birds over each gun and the birds themselves will be high enough to be testing shots for the hunters.

Once the keeper is happy that the drive is complete he blows a whistle or horn and the guns lower and unload their shotguns. No shooting may take place after this signal. The guns, who may well have brought retrieving dogs with them, now set about gathering the birds. The pickers-up who have been standing well behind the line

of guns, collect birds that have fallen some way back or been injured. The beaters help retrieve the birds and they are all carried back to the game cart, and then the process begins again in another area.

A typical day may involve seven or eight separate drives with a break for lunch. At the end of the day the guns and beaters gather to inspect the bag and a pair of birds is given to each gun, the remainder being sold to a game dealer. Game meat can be freely bought and sold in Britain and provides an extra, albeit small, source of revenue for the landowner.

On many shoots, Clarendon Park included, a proportion of the shoot days are sold to outsiders to help cover the costs of running the operation.

becomes particularly onerous when the skill of the guns is unknown. A poor group of guns may require more birds to be put over them than an experienced group, and this can greatly complicate the keeper's job for the day.

A DAY'S HUNTING IN NORTH AMERICA

In contrast to the British system, with its emphasis on intensive management, high numbers and formalised arrangements, most pheasant shooting in North America is conducted by small groups of hunters on a fairly informal basis. This is partly due to the different traditions of hunting. Compared to Europeans, North Americans are

These let days are typically sold on the basis of the number of birds that will be expected to be shot and, even on unsold days, there is often a sweep to guess the number of birds that will be shot that day. A large part of the keeper's skill is therefore to ensure that the guns on that day meet their target number but do not exceed it by very much. Considerable thought goes into deciding which drives will be used on a given day, and when each drive will finish, to ensure that the specified bag is achieved but not exceeded. This

Wetlands provide some of the best pheasant hunting in North Dakota. (John Carroll)

closer to their subsistence hunting roots and a much higher proportion of the population is involved. In some rural states over 50 per cent of the male population hunts at some time during their lives.

The hunting conditions in North America obviously vary enormously from state to state, and it would be futile to describe all the permutations of habitat and management. For the sake of simplicity, let us just consider a day in North Dakota. The south-eastern corner of the state is near the northern limit for decent pheasant populations, and the land is rolling drift prairie. It is farmed mainly for wheat, but this is interspersed with reed-fringed cattail marshes or sloughs. The weather at the opening of the season is often clear and cold by day, with temperatures falling below freezing at night, so drifts of snow are not an uncommon or un-welcome sight for the pheasant hunter.

The season in North Dakota is longer than is typical in most states and runs for ten weeks with a daily limit of two cocks per hunter; hens are strictly protected. However, the pheasant season coincides with that for grey partridge, duck, rabbit and goose. While the pheasant limit may be small, the chance of encountering other species is always there to increase the diversity of the day.

A typical pheasant hunt may start with a group of two, three or four friends meeting at a house before dawn. They then set off in a pick-up truck with dogs, guns, and picnic lunch for a prearranged hunting site. Although the game belongs to the people rather than the landowner, it is still generally necessary to gain the farmer's permission before hunting. In the previous weeks deals will have been made and favours called in to allow access to a farm for the day. Money rarely changes hands in this state, although this is not always true elsewhere. Most hunting access is given as a favour to friends or relatives.

After a drive out in the early light, the hunt starts from the roadside, with the hunters lining up on stubble to walk out towards a wetland. The dogs, often labradors, spaniels or even setters, may work a fenceline or field edge as they go. But the main aim is to get to the isolated reedbeds or wood lots and work them for the game. The clothes, by law, must include a bright 'hunter orange' cap for safety and in many areas a simi-larly coloured jacket is also essential. Jeans, a flannel shirt and good walking boots complete the hunter's wardrobe.

Compared with their British counterparts, American hunters must work for their sport and one or two flushes of single cocks per hour would make a satisfying day. The birds are usually flushed forward of the guns and shot as they fly away or curl to the side, a very different technique to driven shoots where the birds are usually taken as they fly towards the hunter. This is not to say that driving birds is unheard of. If the birds have been hunted hard a few sportsmen may line out at the end of a piece of cover while the others push the game towards them, but drives on the large, formal scale seen in Europe do not occur.

With a stop for a picnic lunch, the hunt may last all day. Most hunters are lucky if they bag their limit of birds; many are more than happy to return home with one bird and two is a bonus. As a consequence, much more time is spent admiring a bird after it is shot than is the case on most driven shoots, and discussions of spurs, colouring and tail length are common. In fact many bars run annual contests to see who can bring in the bird with the longest tail. Under these conditions pheasants can acquire an almost trophy status and particularly impressive birds are often stuffed.

The contrast in hunting techniques, traditions and management between the two continents is enormous. The driven shoot gives emphasis to high densities and the number shot, and makes shooting the preserve of the rich or dedicated. Walked-up shooting makes hunting available to as many people as possible, concentrates on the hunt itself and focuses attention on the individual bird. Both have their advantages and disadvan-tages. Driven shooting provides a direct incentive for the landowner to manage the habitat, but the American system is, to my mind, more aestheti-cally pleasing. Almost the only thing the two systems have in common is the bird they are chasing.

Ageing and measuring shot birds is a useful way of collecting information about populations.

AGEING PHEASANTS

One common topic of conversation at the end of a day's hunting is how one ages a pheasant, if only to ensure that one takes a plump young bird home rather a some stringy old one. The problem is that many methods work – sometimes. Unlike most birds, pheasants undergo a complete moult every year; even juveniles change all of their feathers in the late summer and autumn. The tricks that work for partridge, grouse or woodcock, like looking for old worn wing feathers held over from the previous moult, just do not work for pheasants. Instead most people rely on the length of the male's spurs or the strength of the bones or bill.

Spurs can be quite a good indicator, early in the winter at least, but of course they are no help in ageing hens. Cock birds start to grow their spurs at eight to ten weeks of age. By the start of the shooting season they are still fairly short and rounded in most of the juveniles, but long and sharp in adults. Problems start around December when the biggest juveniles may already have spurs that would do an old rooster proud. From then on it is fairly safe to say that a bird with small spurs is young but big spurs do not necessarily indicate an adult. Selecting a pheasant to take home on the basis of spur length in January could mean that you miss the plumpest young cocks and end up with the runt of the litter.

Bones and bill can also give an indication of age. The idea being that young birds have not finished calcifying these bits. If you pick up a shot bird by its lower bill or one of its legs and it breaks under the bird's weight then the chances are that it is a young one. Although this works with both sexes it becomes less reliable as the winter progresses. It also depends on the weight of the bird and is not much use to a biologist dealing with live birds.

One reliable method is to measure the depth of a small hole that is found about / inch inside the vent. This is where a small organ, known as the Bursa of Fabricius, empties into the gut. Once a bird matures, this organ regresses and the hole all but closes up. It is possible to insert a blunt needle or a thin matchstick into the bird's anus and measure the depth of the canal leading to the Bursa. I spent a long day on a shoot in Wicklow, Ireland measuring this canal on their shot birds to try to discover which of the other, more socially acceptable ageing techniques was most effective. Ten years later I gave a talk to a group of hunters in Dublin. One announced to the audience that I was still remembered in Wicklow as a pheasant molester. And although this method can be tried on live birds I would not recommend it.

Lastly, and probably most effectively, it is possible to look at the shape and size of the main, primary wing feathers. At about five weeks, young pheasants start to shed these and grow the ones that will last them through to the next summer. They have ten of these primary feathers and start by moulting the one nearest to their body. As this feather regrows when the bird is still only half its final size it has a narrow shaft and is generally shorter and narrower than in an adult. By plucking this feather it is fairly easy to separate young from old by eye. It works just as well for both sexes and you can use it, if you need to, right through from September until June. It also looks much more impressive at the end of a day's shooting to count through the wing feathers and, with a flourish, announce that such and such a bird is an adult or juvenile instead of coming armed with your set of blunt needles.

IMPROVING THE FLYING ABILITY OF REARED PHEASANTS

In recent years there has been considerable debate on British pheasant shoots, where the feeling is that the flying ability of the typical reared bird has been declining. As fast, high-flying birds are the main aim of a good pheasant shoot, a decline in quality has been a major worry and many different approaches have been tried to resolve the problem. The difficulty has been that, on many reared pheasant shoots, the birds are thought to have become large, fat and lazy, and when they are pushed over the guns they tend to fly low and slowly.

What could possibly have changed to bring about such widespread concern? It is very difficult to get to grips with a topic like this as there is little hard data on how birds flew before people noticed the problem. Although many hunters and gamekeepers are convinced that things have deteriorated, this is not much help. There are also a great many estates that have tried different solu-tions and swear that such and such a change in management has reversed the trend. The problem is that there seem to be almost as many different solutions as there are estates. All in all it is a difficult subject to research.

What is clear is that the average British pheasant has become heavier in recent decades. For example, in the 1950s scientists weighed shot pheasants on one of our study areas and the cocks averaged 1,335g, the hens 993g. We repeated this process in the mid-1980s by which time the males were 7 per cent heavier at 1,423g and the females 11 per cent heavier at 1,107g. This is an isolated example but seems to hold true across much of the country where pheasants are released. Big birds seem to be found where there is a long history of rearing, while those estates which have relied on wild birds still have small ones.

While many reared pheasants fly superbly, there is an increasing feeling that some are becoming less good at it. (Hugo Straker)

HOW HEAVY IS A TYPICAL PHEASANT?

There is no easy answer to this question; there is an enormous variation depending on which part of the world it is taken from. Moreover, weight is a combination of body size and fatness. The native birds of China seem to be particularly light; hens of around 600g are not at all unusual. I once caught a reared hen in Dorset, England which weighed 1,800g, three times as heavy as the smaller Chinese birds.

Weights also vary within China. Zhang Zheng-wang visited the museums in Beijing and collated the weights of their 128 specimens. He found that male birds in the colder north and west weighed around 1,130g compared to about 970g in the warm south and east. Specially bred strains of birds can also reach extremes of weight. One farmer I know in Cambridgeshire has been selecting a strain of birds for low body weight and has produced a reared pheasant as small as any seen in China, while the Americans have bred commercial strains with cocks of up to 2,500g for the table.

Source	Provenance	Males (g)	Females (g)
China	Native wild	1,066	795
Cambridge, England	wild	1,198	919
Ohio, USA	wild	1,248	993
Michigan, USA	wild	1,275	971
Co Kildare, Ireland	wild	1,288	971
Galloway, Scotland	wild	1,335	1,092
Illinois, USA	wild	1,362	1,078
Nebraska, USA	wild	1,393	1,022
Hampshire, England	reared	1,447	1,097
Dorset, England	reared	1,454	1,122

When I have spoken to hunters and game-keepers about the problem of flying ability, they always return to two points: that the poor flying birds are too big and too tame. The solutions that have been tried have been designed to solve these two problems. Many estates have introduced smaller, wild-type strains of birds to improve flying ability. Others have altered the way they feed the birds to stop them getting fat and have tried to reduce the amount of contact they have with the keeper, hoping to make them warier of humans when it comes to the shoot day. In particular there has been a move away from feeding the birds by hand on straw-covered rides towards the use of hoppers or spreading grain at night so that the birds do not associate humans with food. Many estates try both these things at the same time: a new strain of birds and altered feeding. This makes it particularly hard for us to work out what is important. From a scientific viewpoint we need to change one thing at a time

so that we can judge which has the most effect. Understandably, shoots with a problem cannot wait years for scientists to go through this process, so they try everything at once in the hope that something works, and it sometimes does.

What then do we know about the factors that can make a pheasant a good flier? In the last chapter I touched briefly on work we carried out with Doug Wise in Cambridge, comparing the performance of wild and game-farm strains of birds. The most common approach to declining flying ability has been to introduce a new strain of bird. Apart from comparing the breeding success of the two groups, we also wanted to see if the smaller, wild type birds could improve the quality of the shooting, so we had someone there on each shoot day to see how well the different groups flew.

Measuring a pheasant's flying ability is no easy task. Although most hunters on driven shoots want to see high, fast birds, this is hard to measure and depends on the contours of the ground. To try to get around this we decided to record the angle of take-off to the nearest 10°. So we spent many hours that winter standing next to the guns as the birds were flushed towards them, giving each bird a score on its ability: 1 for a bird that flopped past the guns parallel to the ground and 5 for a scorching climber heading up and up. This led to quite a lot of competition between the guns – 'Did you see that bird I got on the last drive, you should have given that an eight at least . . . what, it can't have only been a three!' Luckily, there were a number of the guns who were also willing to shoot some of the low birds for the sake of our research, something which is frowned upon on most driven shoots. It is worth pointing out that we had no idea which bird was which as they flew past us, as the little metal wing tags that marked the different groups were much too small to see. If a bird was shot we then marked where it fell and raced the dogs to pick it up when the drive was over. Each was weighed and measured and the tag recorded.

We recorded the take off angle and duration of active flight of pheasants on a wide variety of different shoots. (Hugo Straker)

How high each bird flew had a significant effect on whether it was shot at or not. On British driven shoots the guns are usually presented with more than one target at the same time, and there is a strong desire only to shoot at the most challenging birds. This was apparent in our study; the guns chose to shoot at the fastest-climbing birds. Interestingly, their chances of hitting a bird did not change a great deal as the height of the bird increased. This is not to say that high pheasants are easy to hit – far from it – rather that on a flat piece of ground it was rare for the birds to present really challenging targets.

Against this background we then looked to see if the scores of the wild and game-farm birds differed. There was certainly a difference but it was really rather small. On average a game-farm bird took off at 27°, while a wild type managed 30°. To a large extent this was due to the size of the wild-type birds, as there was a general trend for smaller birds to take off at a steeper angle. From this study we concluded that smaller, wild-type birds do fly a bit better than the typical game-farm ones, largely because they are smaller, but that the main thing affecting how well a bird flies is the way the drive is planned and laid out in the first place. Releasing small wild-type birds will not transform a badly planned drive into a good one. But, if the drive is already working well, it may help add a bit more spice to the presentation.

Looking at just one estate and two different types of birds can only scratch the surface of the problem. Despite the small differences we found between the wild and game-farm strains, many hunters felt that we had underestimated the improvements that could accrue from small, wild-type strains, so we set out to visit a wider range of different shoots, visiting each once to see how different management affected flying ability.

Over two winters we recorded the flying ability of birds from about 40 different shoots, some that had released small, wild-type birds, others with typical game-farm stock and the whole range of different feeding methods. This time we measured more than just the angle of take-off, we also counted how many seconds each bird flapped for. Of course, visiting each shoot only once meant that we had to cope with differences in the weather, something that certainly affects the way birds fly. On a dull, windy day the birds fly far more strongly than on a still, clear one, for some reason the birds do not like flying in bright sunshine. We also knew from previous experience that birds fly best when they do not have to fight their way through a dense tree canopy, when they are made to fly across 200–300 yards of open ground to the next piece of cover or if they can see the guns shortly after being flushed. All of these components are certainly important, but, by visiting enough shoots we hoped that their effects would cancel out and let us judge how different management strategies affected flight.

There was considerable variation in how well the birds flew on different shoots. Remember that we were measuring the birds' actual performance, rate of climb and duration of active flight, rather than simply how high they were when they passed over the guns. It was also interesting to see what a small difference in flying ability was necessary to turn a bad drive into a good one. On poor drives, typical birds took off at 20° and flapped for four seconds. On good ones the average was 30° and six seconds. Just 10° and a further two seconds of active flight made a huge difference. The best bird we saw took off at 45° and flapped for 11 seconds.

About a dozen of the shoots we visited had bought in small, wild-type birds. Of the 40 places visited, the best two were ones with these special small birds. In itself this supports the idea that they are better than the average game-farm bird. However, two out of the five worst shoots also had these small, wild-type birds. Overall, those shoots with small, wild-type birds had no better flying quality than average. This does not mean that there is no effect at all. Because of the demand for birds of this sort, there was a number of rather dubious strains for sale. Some which are said to be first-generation birds from wild stock or imported from a country with a reputation for wildness are in fact indistinguishable from ordinary game-farm birds in size and temperament.

We collected a sample of shot birds from each of the shoots we visited and dissected them to see how much fat and muscle they were carrying. To our surprise we found no relationship between the size of the birds and their flying abilities, but there *was* a tendency for the leanest birds to be the best fliers. It also looked as though those birds from verifiable wild strains were the ones least

prone to fatness, regardless of their actual body size. In contrast to our study in Cambridge, which found that small birds flew best, comparing different shoots revealed that leanness was more important.

We also looked at how many birds were flushed on each drive and their average flying ability. This gave us another clear effect; the average bird flew less well on a big drive than on a small one. It was even possible to see the same thing on an individual drive. Those birds that flushed singly tended to fly strongly, while in large groups they tended to go low as if they felt there was safety in numbers.

Where does this leave us? Apart from the obvious effects of weather, drive layout, distance to cover, rolling ground and the visibility of the guns, we also found that lean birds fly best, particularly if they flush in small groups. Releasing small, wild-type birds certainly did not guarantee good fliers, although these birds did tend to be leaner than average. And as in our Cambridge study, we also found that many of the worst-flying birds could be explained by badly laid out drives, rather than a problem with the birds themselves.

Why then should there have been such concerns about declining flying ability? It is hard to be sure, but my feeling is that two things happened in the late 1980s that combined to bring this about. At this time the British economy was going through a boom and there was a considerable demand for pheasant shooting. Many shoots started rearing many more birds than they had in the past. As we found on our shoot visits, a large number of birds on a drive makes for poor individual quality, especially if they flush in big groups. At the same time many commercial game-farms abandoned their tradition of overwintering birds to use as laying stock, relying instead on keepers supplying them with birds caught in the spring or their eggs. These birds have survived the shooting season and are easily caught. They may have consistently flown low through the season so that no one bothered to shoot at them or they may have had large appetites, making them prone to capture in baited traps. It is unsurprising that their offspring shared the same characteristics. I suspect that this combination of increased numbers and breeding from the survivors was responsible for part of the

Some shoots have moved away from regular hand feeding as they feel it may make the birds too tame and less wary of humans. (Hugo Straker)

problem. I doubt whether simply purchasing a wild-type strain will solve most shoots problems. If nothing else, it is hard to get a verified strain any more, and if the same system of catching survivors is used, any benefits will soon be lost. Nevertheless, obtaining new strains of birds does seem to have some benefits, although this must be taken in context. Probably seven out of ten of the drives we observed could have been improved by more careful planning and this is the one thing that is virtually guaranteed to produce substantial results. It is too easy to blame the birds and rely on drives that worked well in the past, without appreciating how every year makes the woodland that much taller and through time changes its ability to produce good birds.

The very worst birds we saw were ones that were obviously overfed, carrying great slabs of fat in their bodies, so it is hardly surprising that they did not fly well. Bad feeding can affect the birds in two ways: apart from making them fat it can also tame them if they are called to the whistle for feeding. Nevertheless, it does seem that certain strains of birds are more prone to becoming fat

than others, and increased numbers of 'fatties' may reflect changes in the strain as much as changes in feeding. Having said that, avoiding maize which can make the birds very fat, and using hoppers or night feeding all seem sensible precautions.

The question of numbers is equally important. Too many birds on a drive can very easily lead to poor quality, so cutting back on numbers should be an effective way of improving quality, although it is obviously expensive. Alternatively, designing the drive so that the birds flush in small groups, in particular using numerous small flushing points and carefully controlling the beaters can avoid the worst of the large flush syndrome.

The ideal bird is one that is small, lean and wild, but more important than that is a shoot manager who puts time into the planning and layout of the drives. The most obvious thing that affected how well the birds flew on the various shoots we visited was the attitude of the owner or gamekeeper. Compared to all the arguments about strain, body size, leanness, wildness, feeding and flushing, nothing compares with putting thought into the way each drive is planned. This is the real secret of making pheasants fly.

MANAGEMENT

A cross Europe and North America pheasants ride on the farmer's coat-tails. Agriculture created the habitat in which they live, man introduced the bird to the countryside and sportsmen try to ensure that they thrive. There is a lot of interest in managing pheasant populations, trying to keep their numbers as high as possible. Understanding the birds' life and requirements is an invaluable starting point from which to look at management, but what can actually be done to improve the stocks of wild birds? Before discussing the details of management it is worth taking a quick look at some areas where things have gone well to see just what can be achieved.

If they are not held back, pheasants can achieve extraordinary densities. The world record for wild pheasants, as far as I know, is held by Pelee Island in Lake Erie. This is in Canadian territory, between Ohio and Ontario, not far from

The habitat and management at Seefeld has helped achieve notably high wild pheasant densities.

Detroit. The island, about 8 miles long and 3fi wide, covers just over 10,000 acres and, in its day, held quite extraordinary numbers of pheasants. Settled in 1834, it was originally an inhospitable place, with almost half the island covered in snake- and mosquito-infested marshland, and the remaining higher ground comprising forest. Gradual drainage and forest clearance turned it into productive farmland and its separation from mainland North America ensured that it remained virtually free of mammalian predators, such as foxes and racoons. Islands also have one other advantage: if nothing kills the animals then the extra young produced each year have nowhere else to go and can build up to spectacular densities.

Although no one is sure when pheasants were first introduced to Pelee they were certainly not common before 1927 when 36 birds were released. After only six years they were so common that the farmers were complaining of crop damage and a hunting season was opened for the islanders. Two years later the season was extended to non-residents in an effort to control their numbers. By 1938, Pelee Island boasted the most liberal hunting regulations in North America: two seasons, each with a limit of 12 birds of which two had to be hens. Although there are no accurate figures for the number of pheasants on the island in its heyday, Allan Stokes, who spent two years studying the Pelee population at the end of the 1940s, estimated five birds per acre in the autumn during the mid- to late 1930s. For a 10,000 acre island this amounts to around 50,000 birds! Pheasants were so common that it was the custom for the islanders to serve them up to visitors and for many families to can pheasants as an extra source of food, particularly during the Great Depression. Even in 1950, when Allan was conducting his studies and pheasant numbers had fallen to a mere 40,000, about 50 per cent of the island's municipal revenue was still generated by the sale of hunting licences. The money brought in by visiting hunters helped the islanders more directly. On his return to the island after the 1950 season, Allan wrote: 'There were signs of pheasant prosperity everywhere. Every house I visited had some major improvement: oil furnace, new bathroom, electricity or new car. These islanders need not be told the value of pheasants.'

I have never had the chance to see a wild pheasant population at anything like the density Allan Stokes encountered on Pelee Island, and I doubt whether such a place now exists. This density was, moreover, the result of a chance combination of good habitat created accidentally by the farmers and a predator-free island environment. To create something even approaching Pelee in more typical circumstances requires real dedication, and the nearest place to it that I have ever seen is in Austria. In 1989 I spoke at a conference in Vienna and, as part of the discussion on managing wild gamebird populations, we were taken to the Seefeld Estate which I have referred to a number of times before, on the border with what was then Czechoslovakia. This 5,000 acre estate is jointly run by Count Alceo Bulgarini and his son, Count Maximilian Hardegg, and has the reputation of being among the best wild pheasant shoots in existence. My first visit was interesting, but gave little idea of just how impressive the estate really was. As I later learned, they kept the delegates away from the best areas to avoid scaring the birds! From what they did say about the numbers of birds, it was still obvious that they had something special. Maximilian, who was then completing his training to take on the running of the estate, started a correspondence and later the next year I had the chance to revisit the area and see just what it had to offer.

I returned to Seefeld in April 1990, the perfect time of year to get an idea of the breeding density. Driving around the land early one morning with the owners and their gamekeeper, Karl Pock, I soon gave up trying to record all the breeding birds. There were just too many; every clump of reeds or piece of scrub seemed to have two or three territories, all with four or five hens. Later counts, when I had more time to write down what I saw, showed that they had the second highest breeding density of wild pheasants on record, at least on the best parts of the estate. Pelee Island had a breeding density of nearly one hen per acre, while the most attractive parts of Seefeld contained about one every two acres.

The estate is blessed with good sandy soils and warm, continental summers, both classic features of the best wild pheasant areas. It also contains a good mixture of woodland, reed beds and arable land, but in all of these factors it is not very different from other farms where pheasants are far less abundant. The border, the old Iron Curtain, ran to the north of the area, a few fields from the edge of the estate, and the undisturbed rough ground it contained was another bonus for the pheasants, providing a quiet refuge for them. However, the success of the pheasant shoot cannot be put down simply to its fortunate climate, topography and position.

The estate was reclaimed from an old marsh (Seefeld actually means 'Sea Field'), and its pheasant population rose to its highest levels in the 1960s through a combination of sympathetic farming, predator control and the fact that it acted as a winter refuge for birds from the surrounding farms. However, the mid-1970s saw Austrian farmers introduce more modern farming techniques: mechanised operations, the widespread use of agricultural pesticides and field enlargement. As with so many other areas that once contained healthy wild pheasant populations, the stock went into a decline. But unlike the majority of farms faced with this dilemma, the owners decided to try and do something about it.

Apart from just continuing with the traditional management techniques and hoping that the birds would recover, or switching to the release of hand-reared birds to maintain the shooting,

they took a more active approach. When I first saw the area, they had been making very effective use of the liberal Austrian regulations for set-aside, together with some imaginative use of the need to conserve water stocks for their irrigation system. While the rest of Europe was struggling with the restrictive cutting and planting regulations of set-aside in the European Community, Austria allowed some imaginative uses of their surplus land. In particular, at Seefeld the owners had developed a system of sowing an unharvestable mixture of cereals, rape, sunflowers, maize and other crops on their set-aside land. They replanted half of each field in strips every second year, giving them an intimate mixture of newly sown and older areas. This produced the equivalent of an extremely weedy cereal field mixed in with areas of taller standing cover from the previous year, full of spring forage, nesting sites, chick-food insects and quite respectable winter cover for the birds. Whether this was entirely in line with the original guidelines from the Austrian government remains

The Seefeld set-aside, with its mix of tall and low cover, provides a haven for pheasants and other wildlife.

uncertain, but it met the spirit, if not the letter of the law. The value of their initiative in developing this system should not be underestimated. After considerable lobbying something very like it was finally introduced into the British set-aside regulations as The Wild Bird Cover Option in 1993. It is also not a question of just helping pheasants; their set-aside was teeming with insects of every sort, and smaller birds busily feeding themselves and their chicks.

In combination with this, the dry north Austrian summers demanded an efficient water conservation system if their irrigation was to be effective. Rather than just creating a number of sterile-water storage lagoons, they had dug intricate ponds next to some of the best pieces of existing pheasant habitat. Water has a great effect on the development of attractive pheasant habitat in dry climates, and the creation of these ponds had a big influence on the distribution of reed and shrubs, both good things to have around if one wants to increase wild pheasant stocks. These two approaches had a real effect on the pheasant populations. Unlike other Austrian farms, they had managed to halt the birds' decline and were able to maintain a viable wild pheasant shoot in combination with a profitable farm. They used their agricultural expertise to develop both the set-aside mixture and a sympathetic method of water storage. Modern agriculture had paid to reverse its own most detrimental effects.

My job is not to act as a game adviser and I spend far less time than I would like visiting estates. However, the success of the Seefeld Estate and the healthy wild pheasant stocks they had been able to maintain meant that I wanted to keep in touch with their work to see what I could learn. A steady series of visits over the next few years, often in the company of other staff from the Game Conservancy Trust, identified a few other things they could improve: better management of their woodlands, planting more of their set-aside mix and digging more ponds (which I am sure they would have done anyway), the more sympathetic use of pesticides on their arable crops, feeding their birds throughout the spring, and a system of monitoring the response of their pheasant population to see what worked best. But this was just icing on the cake; the preservation of their stock is due to their own initiative.

One of the things that interests me most about working on pheasants is the ability the birds have to influence the way in which farmers and landowners manage their land, to the benefit of a whole range of wildlife. I cannot think of a better example of how this principle works than to stand on the border of Seefeld. It is full of small reed-fringed ponds, carefully preserved and managed woodlands, and plots of their diverse set-aside. This compares with the neighbouring farms where there is nothing but intensive agriculture; with the odd plot of neatly mown, and virtually sterile, standard set-aside.

DENSITY DEPENDENCE

It is clear that pheasants can build up to high densities, either on their own as on Pelee Island, or with man's help as at Seefeld. It is also obvious that high pheasant populations are the result of favourable conditions. But even in the best areas the number of birds seems to reach an upper limit, and understanding what limits pheasant numbers is the key to successful management. What controls the number of births and deaths? How does hunting influence the population? And what can be done to increase the stocks?

How can we understand the way different factors interact to limit the number of pheasants in an area?

Pheasants, like all plants and animals, have the potential to increase their numbers at a phenomenal rate. A stock of one pair of pheasants could, in theory, become 15,000 birds in just five years if there were no deaths. This potential is of course never realised, although some populations have still managed to increase at an amazing rate. In the mid-1930s six pheasants were introduced to Protection Island in Washington and five years later there were around 1,700 of them – well below the maximum increase possible, but still very respectable. Given this dramatic potential for increase, why do most pheasant populations stay stable or, in many cases, decline? The hens do not seem to produce fewer eggs as numbers increase; clutch size and hatchability seem to remain remarkably constant in high- and low-density populations. If it is not the birth rate that is dropping, therefore it must be that deaths are increasing.

Despite early models of pheasant populations, their numbers appear to be limited by more than just the quality of the habitat.

The death of one pheasant seems to increase the survival prospects of the remainder. (David Hill)

In the 1930s an American quail biologist, Paul Errington, suggested an explanation that, at first sight, is very attractive. His idea is commonly known as the doomed surplus, and although it was a great advance in our knowledge at the time, it has since caused a lot of problems. The theory, as far as pheasants are concerned, runs roughly as follows. Imagine a field with ten bushes in it, each bush big enough for one pheasant to hide under. Predators hunt in the field and will kill any pheasant that is not safely hidden under a bush. Every now and again a big winter storm also kills any pheasant not hidden. What then is the limit to the number of pheasants that can ever live in this area? The answer is obvious: ten, one under each bush. Introduce a pair of pheasants to this area and it will increase until all the bushes are taken; after that predators and bad weather will kill any extra birds produced, the doomed surplus.

The beauty of this argument was that it justified hunting and the tolerance of predators. Shooting was only removing birds that would have been killed by predators or bad weather. It would not have endangered the population, which was limited by the number of bushes, in other words habitat quality.

Errington's idea was very attractive, simple, convenient and, in many cases, easy to translate into management. Its implications are that creating the right habitat is the only way of increasing the stock; predator control is pointless as predators are only killing birds that would have died for some other reason. For the same reason, shooting should not reduce the population as long as enough birds are left to use the available habitat.

The doomed surplus theory held sway for many years, and its management conclusions still carry a lot of weight in some areas. Unfortunately, life is not so simple. Another model of the regulation of populations comes closer to explaining how things actually seem to work. Known as density-dependent regulation it says that there is no single factor limiting bird numbers, like the number of bushes in the doomed surplus theory. As numbers increase, each bird becomes more vulnerable to a whole range of different threats and overall mortality increases until it gets to the point that the number of deaths equals the number of births and the population levels out.

This theory can be illustrated by an analogy. Imagine a pond with fish that like to live near the bottom, where their food is most abundant. As the fish multiply some of them are forced to live nearer and nearer the surface where food is relatively scarce. Life at the surface is dangerous, because not only is there less food but there are also herons that will pick the fish off. If the pond ices over, some of them may freeze. The pond also contains weed and the fish use it to hide from the herons. In a case like this, what is it that determines how many fish are in the pond? There is no simple answer, sometimes it will be one thing and sometimes another. If a pair of fish is introduced into an empty pond they will start off doing well and spread until they cover the whole of the bottom of the pond. Some will be taken by the herons, but the water is deep and there are lots of weeds so the fish are relatively safe. As their numbers increase further, some of them have to live nearer the surface and the herons start to pick them off in increasing numbers. Eventually they eat so many that it balances the number of new fish being born and the population stabilises at a certain depth. When the pond freezes it sometimes kills some fish, in which case the numbers gradually increase back up to the original level. At other times the fish manage to breed particularly well and some are forced further towards the surface to become easy prey for the herons, which pushes the population back down.

The level at which the fish population stabilises is determined by a number of interacting factors. The predators are the main cause of death but they are only good at catching fish near the surface. Even then the amount of weed (think of it as habitat quality) can let some fish live near the surface and still be hidden. If food is short the fish may sometimes have to go near the surface to feed, which will also make them more vulnerable. The weather then introduces an unpredictable element to the whole thing. Sometimes it makes them breed well and forces some near to the surface, at other times it kills a proportion of them, depending on how hard it freezes.

This model has a number of implications. A fish's worst enemy is another fish. More fish means less food, more time near the danger zone of the surface and a higher chance of being caught, frozen or starved to death. It also makes for more opportunities for management. Giving the fish extra food means that more of them can stay safe at the bottom, more weed (habitat) means that the population can rise, while discouraging the herons will have a direct effect on mortality and allow the population to move higher in the pond. But no matter what is done there will still be a limit to how many fish the pond can hold. Eventually they will eat all the food, conditions will become so crowded that disease will start to become a serious cause of loss, or the weather will keep killing off the most vulnerable.

This also has different implications for the effects of fishing or hunting. Rather than just killing fish that would have died for some other reason, fishing will add to the total mortality. It will therefore reduce the stock to some extent, but it will also give the survivors more food and more weed to hide behind, and allow them to live nearer the bottom, thereby helping their chances of survival. This is known as partial compensation. So killing animals certainly means fewer will be left but it increases the survival prospects for the remainder, fewer of which will die from other causes.

Of course, neither the doomed surplus nor the less interestingly named density dependent regulation theory is really the way that populations work, but I believe that the latter is a bit more realistic, and is useful when it comes to trying to manage populations. How then do different factors influence pheasant populations and work together to control the stocks?

PREDATORS

It is all too easy to underestimate the role of predation. Despite working with pheasants for 12 years, I have never seen a pheasant being killed by another animal. I have seen them interact with foxes, but never be killed by one. In fact, most of the times that I have seen foxes and pheasants together in the same field, neither has seemed particularly concerned about the presence of the other. Only once have I seen a fox attack a pheasant, jumping out of a thick hedge to land in the middle of a harem of hens feeding around a territorial cock – it missed. When I was in Ireland I even spent one day a month for a whole year

scouring the estate for fox droppings and then sorting through their contents to see how many had been eating pheasants. I found that only about one dropping in 30 contained even a trace of pheasant. Berries, insects, rabbits, mice and rats were all more important in the fox's diet than pheasants. With only this evidence to go on it would be all too easy to assume that foxes and pheasants actually got on quite well and that predation must really be a very unimportant problem in the bird's life.

It was following a group of released birds that first brought home to me just how important the fox is. I had tagged a couple of hundred young birds with large numbered wing-tags and released them from a pen to see how far they moved, and why and when they died. This was my very first experience of working with pheasants and I very quickly noticed that birds were disappearing at an alarming rate. I started searching the bushes and hedgerows near to my pen to look for remains and soon came across numerous bits of wing, tail feathers and wing-tags, all bearing the unmistakable marks of fox teeth. I even borrowed a fox skull from the university to check that the teeth marks fitted. Searching every inch of the dense thorn and bramble thickets near my pen was not easy. As I had sold my motorbike to pay my ferry to Ireland, I took to wearing my old leather jacket, thick gloves and balaclava as I crawled through these areas on my hands and knees. The farm shepherd was especially puzzled by the fact that I had apparently lost a motorbike in the middle of a bramble thicket!

Over three years I released a total of 446 pheasants and found over 200 sets of pheasant remains, usually within the first two months after release. These were just the ones I found; by playing with various statistics I estimated that about 85 per cent of the birds I released ended up being eaten by foxes within a year and that, after three years of releases I had only five left in the area. I left with a very strong impression of how important the fox is for the pheasant but, as I learned from looking at their droppings, how unimportant the pheasant is for the fox.

Working with released birds is one thing, as they are renowned for their stupidity and the ease with which they fall prey to every possible hazard. But studies of wild pheasant populations come to just the same conclusion, although to a lesser extent. The best studies of purely wild pheasant populations come from North America. These are usually from areas where the hens are protected from shooting, but even so they usually show that 60–80 per cent of young hens die each year, with only slightly higher survival rates amongst older birds. The vast majority of deaths are also usually attributable to predation. For instance, in a long-term radiotracking study in Wisconsin, 86 per cent of all deaths were due to predators; shooting, hay mowing, road accidents and starvation were all minor causes of loss. So even in wild pheasant populations, losses each year are considerable and the direct cause of death is usually predation.

In Britain, foxes are the main predator of pheasants. (Malcolm Brockless)

This brings me to the question of predator control. If predators are the main cause of pheasants meeting an untimely end, then surely the way to increase pheasant stocks is to kill the predators. The answer is often yes, but there is more to wildlife management than having large numbers of pheasants. And simply saying that the

direct cause of a bird's death was predation ignores the factors that may have made the bird vulnerable in the first place. Killing predators in sufficient numbers does often lead to an increase in pheasant populations but at what cost, and are there other ways of limiting the effects of predation?

By collecting fox droppings and sorting through the contents, we can build up a picture of the role of pheasants and other animals in their diet. This dropping actually contained a pheasant wing tag, simplifying the process of identification. (Jonathan Reynolds)

I am a great believer in the proposition that man has so changed his environment that he has landed himself with the responsibility for its management, not just for his own good but for the good of the other species that share it with him. Of course it is impossible to conserve everything, everywhere at all times; we have to decide what we want and manage the land and the wildlife it contains to achieve this aim. In some cases this means preserving what nature intended without our interference. Tropical rain forests are a particularly apt example of where we should protect a habitat from our own actions. But we should not forget that much of the world's surface has already been changed out of all recognition by man and that we must take responsibility for these areas as well as the pristine environments that we have not got around to yet.

Pheasants are a species of man-made habitats, at least in their European and North American ranges. The same is true of their main predators. For instance, foxes, crows and many other predators probably reach higher densities on farmland than they would in natural habitats. Man has created alternative food sources for the predator – foxes, for example, now reach their highest recorded densities in some of our cities, where our own refuse is a major part of their diet. We have also exterminated many of the predators' own natural enemies. In North America it appears that removing coyotes allows fox numbers to increase. So removing one top predator can actually let a smaller predator thrive and increase the predation pressure on game. Similarly, the lack of goshawks throughout much of Britain means that one of the crow's main enemies is missing from the system. We must decide what sort of balance we want.

Unlike the dense forest that once covered much of Europe, as here in Bieloweiza National Park in Poland, modern farmland is a man-made habitat and does not have the natural balance found in pristine environments.

This sort of decision could of course be left to nature. In a natural environment there may well be a balance between predators and their prey, but that would mean letting Britain revert to woodland or midwestern America to undisturbed prairie. While both might appeal to the conservationist ideal, I do not consider either to be a sensible option; man is also part of the environment.

Before discussing the effects of predator control on pheasant stocks it is worth considering what has happened in the past, when game managers have tried to remove them. In the late nineteenth century British game shooting was at its peak. The farmland areas were managed for partridge and pheasant, the moorlands were managed for grouse. In all cases the main management technique was to kill anything with sharp teeth, a hooked beak or pointed claws. Gamekeeper numbers reached an all-time high and in some parts of the country there was hardly a parish that was not covered by one or more keepers. This all made for classic game shooting,

but also took a toll on many of our predatory species. Rather than just limiting their effects on the favoured game species, this level of attention led to the extinction of a number of predators and the severe restriction of the ranges of others. Red kites, buzzards, hen harriers, goshawks, fish eagles, pine martens, polecats and wild cats all suffered in this way. Although the precise cause of their demise is open to debate, it was not just due to gamekeepers; the rapid changes in land use that coincided with the increasing interest in shooting certainly played a role. Nevertheless, there can be little doubt that persecution had a significant effect. Is this sort of change really justifiable for the sake of increasing the densities of a few gamebirds? The answer I think is no, but this does not mean that I am against controlling predators, provided it does not endanger their own status.

The two words to note are 'control' and 'status'. A system of predator control that limits the effects of predation should first consider why predation is such a problem in the first place. If the conclusion really is that there are too many predators, it should then seek to limit their influence by humane methods that are unlikely to lead to a

A well-managed piece of land can provide better conditions for both predators and their prey than an intensively farmed area.

restriction in the range or future prospects of the species concerned. For instance, the fact that released pheasants are particularly vulnerable to predators does not justify the extermination of pine martens in England. The problem lies with the released birds rather than the effect of pine martens on their survival. Similarly, the killing of released pheasants by buzzards has been shown to be heavily influenced by the quality of the habitat into which the birds are released. Finding that pheasants released into an inappropriate habitat are killed by buzzards does not justify the latter's persecution. It just shows that more care should have been applied by the game manager, it is his fault, not the buzzards'. However, where a predator is known to be abundant, and its abundance is probably due to man's actions in the first place, as with foxes around the edges of suburbia or magpies near farmyards, then the limited control of the species involved seems entirely justified to me. Man has created the environment which has increased the density of predators. There is no natural balance, so it is up to man to determine what balance is desirable, provided it only reduces the abundance of the predator and their effects on the game, without leading to local or national extinctions. It is also worth bearing in mind that habitat management for game can increase the numbers of many other species as well, including predators. Arguably an area where the habitat is well managed can sustain more predators, even with some degree of control, than an unmanaged, unkeepered piece of ground.

Does predator control work? Certainly the best pheasant areas are ones where predators are either controlled by man, as at Seefeld, or where they are scarce, as on islands such a Pelee or parts of the American Midwest in the 1930s and 1940s And these are not isolated cases; I cannot think of a really high-density wild pheasant population in an area that did not have depressed levels of predators. But although this sort of observation is interesting, it is not proof that predator control works. For this we have to look at areas before and after the introduction of keepering.

Experiments to study the effects of predator control are fairly rare. The best one I know of was carried out for partridges on Salisbury Plain in Wiltshire over seven years, starting in 1985. The idea was to take two similar areas; control foxes, crows, rats, stoats and weasels in one area for three years and then repeat the process in the other area for the next three years, keeping everything else constant. The partridge stock in both areas was counted each year, and also a year before the experiment started. The results were clear: autumn partridge numbers trebled in the areas with predator control, and fell again when predator control ceased.

The predator control experiment on Salisbury Plain found that predation can limit both the size and productivity of partridge populations. (Jonathan Reynolds)

This is fairly conclusive as regards partridges, but does the same hold true for pheasants? When the Salisbury Plain experiment finished Malcolm Brockless, a professional partridge keeper who had carried out the actual predator control, was able to apply his skills to a broader range of techniques on the Loddington Estate in Leicestershire.

This 822 acre estate was owned by Lord and Lady Allerton and after their deaths they left it in trust. Malcolm was employed by the Allerton Trust as part of a project to demonstrate the possibilities of combining sympathetic game management with conservation and profitable farming. Unlike the Salisbury Plain work, this was not a true experiment, more of a demonstration, and predator control was not the only thing that was introduced to the estate. However, it was an area where pheasants formed the most numerous game species. From an autumn stock of 126 birds in 1992, before management began, a single year of predator control and more sympathetic farming methods saw a rise to 303, increasing to an autumn stock of at least 442 birds in 1995. This was at a time when the woodland management had not had time to really benefit the pheasant stock, so the results can be attributed primarily to Malcolm's efforts at predator control and the more sympathetic farming that had been introduced. From the farming viewpoint this has involved the careful use of pesticides to create Conservation Headlands around the cereals, and breaking up some of the larger fields to produce a more mixed crop pattern. The changes are beneficial in themselves but are unlikely on their own to have produced the dramatic response in the pheasant population.

Another predator control experiment was carried out in South Dakota. Two separate types of control were carried out, each for five years. In one case just foxes were controlled while the other involved a range of other mammals as well. Compared with areas where there was no predator control, the fox control area saw a 19 per cent increase in autumn pheasant numbers, and in the area where other mammals were also controlled, populations rose by 132 per cent. After five years, the autumn stock was 338 per cent higher on the latter area while the stocks on the comparable areas with no predator control had also risen, but only by 53 per cent.

There are also other studies, less well designed, from an experimental point of view, but still of interest. In an attempt to stop the spread of rabies from Germany into Denmark, intensive fox control was carried out on a belt of land in southern Jutland from 1964–1974. In this area the bags of pheasants, hares and partridges doubled compared to adjacent areas with no fox control. When fox control ceased in 1975 bags returned to normal, but again increased after 1979 when fox control was once again started.

The evidence is therefore that predator control can increase the productivity of pheasant populations and raise autumn densities. The precise effects on spring numbers are less clear, at least from an experimental viewpoint. But comparing pheasant populations around the world, there is hardly a case where high breeding populations have been achieved without the reduction of predators, either through control or their absence from certain offshore islands.

OLD HENS

Many people who manage wild pheasants express concern about too many old hens. This seems to be a widespread worry based on the fear that old birds will chase the young ones out of an area and may have become too old to breed properly. There is an element of truth in this, as old hens are usually dominant and, in certain circumstances just prior to a decline, populations do seem to have an increased proportion of old birds. However, the decline is not the fault of the old birds; if anything they breed better than inexperienced younger ones. Comparisons of the egg production rates of young and old hens clearly show that the old birds produce more eggs and stay in lay longer than young ones. Our own radiotracking and tagging results also show that they are more likely to rear a successful brood.

The position becomes clearer if the question is rephrased. Instead of 'Why do populations at risk have lots of old birds?' it should be 'Why do they have so few young ones?' This makes everything much easier to understand, and the answers are fairly obvious. The population is at risk of decline because something is stopping the birds producing many young. Even the experienced old hens are finding it hard to rear a brood. Rather than worrying about the old hens the solution is to see what else has changed. A decline in habitat quality, increased predation or changing farming practice with more use of pesticides are the usual culprits. Provided there is a steady input of young into a population there should never be a preponderance of old birds. Even if there is it is not a problem in itself, rather a symptom of some other, underlying cause for concern.

HABITAT QUALITY.

Habitat ranks very high as a reason why some areas have more pheasants than others. 'Think Habitat' say the stickers from Pheasants Forever, the largest sportsman's organisation for this bird in the USA. This is all very well, but what is habitat, and which bits are important?

When I first started work on pheasants in Ireland, my supervisor, John Whelan, took me out to my study area, sat me down and gave me a huge pile of scientific papers to read. I am still amazed at how much work has been done on pheasants over the last 50 years. There are over 600 articles, reports and papers all giving details of some study into their life. The vast majority of these come from North America – probably 75 per cent of the total – and my first few days of reading left me fairly bemused. What, for instance, did they mean by upland nesting cover (in Europe, upland usually means mountainous), tame hay, sloughs and creek bottomland? The farming they described was dominated by corn (by which I later realised they meant maize not cereals, which they call small grains), alfalfa (our lucerne), milo and sorghum. Even the predators they were dealing with meant nothing to me: great horned owls, red-tailed hawks, skunks, racoons and coyotes. All in all I found it very hard to get a proper impression of what they were saying.

Sitting reading papers is all very well but to make sense of this wealth of studies there is nothing better than seeing the land; it is the only way to get a real feel for what is going on. So at the start of my studies in the early 1980s the vast majority of the literature really made very little sense to me. It was not until 1991 that I got my first chance to visit the USA. The Utah Department of Natural Resources was holding a pheasant workshop in Salt Lake City and invited me to speak. I arrived in early January for a four-day visit, together with David Hill with whom I had worked on pheasants in the past, thinking that at last I would get an idea of what American pheasant habitat actually looks like. Unfortunately I had not realised that northern Utah is under deep snow for much of the winter. The Wasatch Front along the edge of the Great Salt Lake also suffers from terrible temperature inversions, creating thick fog that can last for weeks. The conference was interesting and just talking to American game managers cleared up a lot of my problems in understanding their systems.

David and I also visited Utah State University to give a talk to their College of Natural Resources. There we were hosted by John Bissonette, a professor, who showed us some of the beautiful scenery in the mountains, once we got above the fog. He also told us about a scholarship scheme run by the College which would pay for visiting scientists to come and work there for a few months.

When I got back home I set about applying and they agreed to pay my wages for four months and to fly my family out to Salt Lake in early 1993. We arrived to the same snow and fog that I had seen two years earlier, but with four months at my

What differences are there between the ecology of European and North American pheasants?

149

disposal I could afford to wait. The first thing that struck me was how little cover there was for the birds in many areas. Although the rivers and streams were often surrounded by reeds, dogwood and willow scrub, the majority of the farmland was just a white desert with nothing but teasels sticking up above the snow. As the snow thawed after six weeks, I began to get a better idea of the farming, and the loan of a truck from the Department of Natural Resources enabled me to get out and really see the country.

One of the most striking things about American work on pheasants, for a European at least, is the emphasis they give to nesting cover. Report after report describes how many nests were found in different crop types. There are extensive experiments with penned birds looking at which of a variety of grass the birds prefer to nest in, state-sponsored schemes to grow nesting cover along roadsides, studies of the humidity in pheasant nests, and a great deal more. I could never understand why they considered nesting habitat so important. It goes without saying that having somewhere for the birds to nest is important, but our own advisory service and the research that

we were involved with both gave nesting habitat a fairly low priority. Our approach was to get the winter and territory cover right, keep predation under control and make sure there was food for the chicks and adults, and we believed that the birds would look after themselves when it came to nesting. One of the things I really wanted to get to grips with was why the Americans considered nesting cover so vital. Was their farming really so different that there was nowhere to nest? Were the birds actually different from our own? Did their system of land ownership and state-controlled hunting mean that planting nesting habitat was all they could do? Had we got it all wrong and underestimated how important nesting cover really was all along?

I was lucky to meet one of the wildlife rangers, George Wilson, who filled me in on a lot of the background to managing pheasants in the area and showed me around the best spots. George was responsible, almost single-handedly, for pheasant management over the northern part of the state, an area about the size of Wales. Against this background, he had achieved a great deal. In many areas he had relied on planting large blocks of nesting cover where a farmer was willing to take his land out of production. But, on land actually owned by the Department, he had been planting shrubs and getting to grips with

In cold winters, most Utah farmland is hidden beneath a blanket of snow and little pheasant cover can be seen.

the sort of fine-scale management I was more familiar with.

His results were mixed. I particularly remember two large blocks of nesting cover, a couple of hundred acres each, that did not hold a single breeding bird. At the other extreme, the Ogden Nature Center, a little piece of wildlife habitat squeezed in between the town's tax office and an army base, on which he had lavished particular care, was heaving with birds.

I was determined to try to make sense of these differences and relate them to what we already knew about pheasants in Europe. Armed with George's suggestions, a group of volunteers organised by Dean Mitchell and Dave Larson at the Department's headquarters, and the loan of a truck, I set off to try to find out why some places held more birds than others.

What I wanted was to get an idea of the breeding density on as many different blocks of land as I could by counting cocks on their

In Utah, much of the best habitat, cattail marsh and scrub, is concentrated along the river bottoms.

territories and the number of hens with each. Once I had this I could then look to see which habitat features were associated with good breeding densities. As hen pheasants do not seem to move far from their cock's territory to nest, the number seen on the territories should be pretty much the same as the number trying to nest in the area. Between us we ended up counting and surveying 70 square miles of northern Utah and finding big differences in the numbers of birds in each. Some square miles did not hold a single bird, many just held two or three, while George's own favourite plot at the Ogden Nature Center came out top with around 50 birds even though half of the area was concrete.

If nesting cover was the most important thing

We carried out counts of breeding birds from vehicles in the spring.

The edges of shrubs seem to be a favoured habitat for pheasant territories throughout their native and introduced range, as here in North Dakota. (John Carroll)

for pheasants then I should have found the highest breeding densities in areas rich in quality nesting cover: residual vegetation from the previous year's growth, fields of alfalfa, strips of rough grass etc. If, however, something else was important then I should be able to pick that up too. The first thing I did was to look at the places where cock birds set up their territories. Just as in Britain these were typically placed on the edges of shrubby cover, bordering on open agricultural land. Although the birds were closely tied to shrubs, they did not seem to prefer any particular crop type in the neighbouring field. Certainly they were not concentrating on those that might have been attractive for nesting. The next thing was to look at why some squares held more birds than others. I came up with one clear answer, the length of shrubby edge; a lot of it meant plenty of sites for territories and plenty of hens deciding that it was a good spot to try to breed. Nesting cover just did not come into it. I tried all sorts of different measures of how much suitable nesting cover there was to see if it would fit, but nothing did. Finding a lot of birds in April did not seem to have anything to do with the availability of nesting cover but a lot to do with the amount of shrub. As the hens do not move far from the territory to lay their eggs, it also implied that the number nesting in an area had nothing to do with

Just how important is nesting cover, like this switchgrass plot in Pennsylvania, to pheasants in North America? (John Carroll)

the amount of nesting cover that they might find.

This set me thinking. The pile of papers I had been given by John Whelan when I first started work on pheasants had contained dozens of reports describing the density of nests in different habitats. Perhaps these would give me another way of seeing how important nesting cover really was. Back at the University, I set about taking them all out of the library and collating the information. If nesting cover was really important then I should find that areas with lots of good nesting sites would have more birds that those poor in nesting cover. To my surprise I found the same thing from the American literature as I had from my own pheasant counts. The best pheasant densities were found in areas with plenty of shrub, not in ones where there was abundant nesting cover. In fact, the most attractive nesting cover, strips of residual grass, was the one most common on places with low pheasant densities. The nesting studies and the breeding counts both showed the same thing.

These findings were pretty much the same as we had already found in Britain. The number of hens attempting to breed in an area depends on shrubs and the number of cock territories, not on nesting cover. The interesting thing was that the same seemed to be true in North America, in Utah at least.

This is not to say that planting nesting cover is a waste of time, just that it is only worthwhile under certain circumstances. Of course it makes sense to provide safe nesting areas. This is one of the most dangerous times of the year for the birds

and a well-hidden nest site can reduce the chances of predation. However, it seems as though this is all that planting nesting cover can do: it makes the birds safe and more likely to hatch off a brood, it does not increase the number of birds that nest in the area as a whole. If one wants to increase the number of birds that are going to settle, then the thing seems to be to increase the number of suitable territories. These are what the hens are looking for when they move out of their winter covers, and they will chose one without the slightest consideration of where they might later nest. Planting nesting cover only makes sense if there are already sites for territories in the area. This was what was wrong with some of the large nesting blocks I saw in Utah. They did not contain a single bird because they had been planted too far away from the nearest territory. Moreover, it only makes sense to plant nesting cover near to existing territories so that the hens are likely to use them. It is interesting that one American biologist, who was reviewing the success of various schemes to provide nesting cover, said that these programmes only worked when pheasants were already abundant, and did not help when the birds were scarce. In other words, providing nesting cover can help a population that already has the use of many territories, but makes no sense in isolation.

This may seem like splitting hairs. Does it really matter whether planting shrubs or nesting cover is the best way of helping pheasants? I think the answer is very clearly yes. In the early 1980s various state wildlife agencies were spending over $36 million a year on planting nesting cover to try and increase their pheasant stocks. The amount they spent on shrub planting is best conveyed by the fact that they did not bother to include it on the survey forms. The money available to restore game and wildlife populations is limited, and money spent unwisely is money lost.

Why should so many North Americans have decided that nesting cover was so important? I think part of the reasons stems from the nature of the areas they work in. The best North American pheasant populations seem to be in the Midwest, areas that are fairly open and where, although the birds do not reach particularly high densities compared to Pelee Island or Seefeld, they achieve respectable numbers over very wide areas. In these states the territories are fairly diffuse, and the shortage of shrubs means that cocks often set them up on the edges of standing grass, reeds or the like. The density of territories or of hens is not particularly high but these conditions go on for hundreds of miles so the total pheasant population is huge. In the winter the birds are hard pressed to find protection from the elements and large numbers will often congregate in relatively small patches of cover, ideal conditions for hunters. In this way the best pheasant states are classified by the hunting opportunities and total number of birds shot, rather than the actual densities of birds breeding in the area. Good pheasant states often do not seem to hold particularly high breeding densities, they just have so much land with moderate densities that, when concentrated by the winter weather, it looks as though they have huge numbers of birds. The numbers are large, but the densities are often low.

The best example of this pattern that I came across was in Idaho. A sportsman with a keen interest in pheasants took me to see his favourite hunting area. It turned out to be a small patch of shrub and reeds in the middle of a huge, fairly boring sea of farmland. Every winter he was guaranteed his daily limit of pheasants by visiting this one area, so in hunting terms it was ideal pheasant habitat. What it really contained was the only patch of winter cover for miles around, surrounded by land that could only hold modest breeding densities. The habitat was not particularly good for pheasants, it was just good for hunting.

It strikes me that many people in both North America and Europe are judging their pheasant stocks by the quality of the hunting, which is fair enough. But if they decide on this basis that they must therefore have an ideal pheasant breeding habitat, they have jumped to the wrong conclusion.

I spent a couple of days touring pheasant habitat in Kansas with Kevin Church, who worked for their Wildlife and Parks Service. Kansas has an excellent reputation for pheasant hunting but we saw only modest breeding densities, lower even than in parts of Utah, which is viewed as marginal pheasant country. What Kansas had was miles and miles of the same thing while in Utah the pheasant habitat was very localised. As a result Kansas could claim a huge total pheasant population, but one that was fairly thinly spread over an enormous area. Kevin and I looked for territories and, as often as not, when we found one it was in an area with a few shrubs at its heart. We also saw areas where there was not a shrub to be seen and cocks wandering around away from any visible cover. When this happened we were almost certain to be in an area with a particularly low breeding density. Even in Kansas it looked as though the better pheasant densities were associated with shrubs, but there were so few shrubs that it was not obvious unless one was looking for it.

Another thing that has put a lot of North Americans off planting woody cover is confusion about the sort of things that are needed. In Kansas I saw the result of one such scheme, which had funded the planting of rows of conifers to act as shelter during their hard winters. Young conifers are good for pheasants; they provide dense windproof cover, and they become established and grow quickly. The problem is that they do not stop growing. While a 6 or 7 foot high conifer is ideal for the winter and as territory cover, a 30 foot high one is bare and windswept underneath and provides nothing more than perches for great horned owls and red-tailed hawks, both serious pheasant predators. In Kansas they had stopped planting woody cover as a result.

The same problem has arisen in Pennsylvania, although for a different reason. Here, land abandoned from agriculture rapidly fills up with multiflora rose, a lovely shrub species for pheasants although the farmers hate it. In time this is followed by oak which, combined with high deer densities, eventually forms a bare, closed canopy high forest, which is anathema to pheasants although it is ideal for turkeys. John Carroll and I

toured one of his study areas where the local Pheasants Forever chapter were trying to raise the pheasant stock. The area was certainly not short of woody cover, so why was it not full of pheasants? The thing was that the woody cover was all high forest, with not a shrub to be seen, and it was full of the predators that thrive on perches. Thirty or so years ago, when the local pheasant population was at its peak, these woods would have provided abundant shrubby cover for the birds, but now they were death-traps and the pheasants sensibly avoided them like the plague. John was working closely with the local hunters and together they had drawn up a management plan that incorporated a whole range of different strategies to help the birds. They were fencing cattle away from the streams to allow tall grass and shrubs to regenerate, planting shrubs where necessary, cutting the edges of their woodlots to encourage shrubby regrowth and planting plots of nesting cover close to the territories – in all a well-rounded and profitable approach.

The trick is to differentiate between shrubby cover and woodland. In an area where there are lots of birds of prey, pheasants will avoid living next to tall trees. This is why British birds do not seem to mind tall trees; we hardly have any birds of prey big enough to kill adult pheasants. This does not mean that pheasants do not like shrubs in North America, just that it is important not to let low shrubby cover develop into tall trees. 'Think habitat' is a fine motto, but it is important not to think that nesting cover is the be-all and end-all of pheasant management.

The British have also gone off on the wrong tack, although for different reasons. With our

In the winter many birds can concentrate in relatively small patches of cover.

Shrubs at the centre of a pheasant territory in Kansas.

reliance on reared birds that are released in the autumn and, to a large extent, have vanished by the spring, the emphasis has been on providing winter cover. Just as the Americans are world leaders in designing what to plant to help nesting birds, the British are, I think, the best at winter cover. The problem is that the two do not get together or consider the other things that wild pheasants need.

From what I have described in earlier chapters I hope it is now fairly clear that pheasants need a variety of different habitats at different times of year: winter cover, territory sites, nesting areas and brood-rearing habitat. If they are to build up

In many parts of Pennsylvania, the woodlots have become overgrown and provide little shrubby cover for pheasants.

In other areas, low shrubby areas remain, or are being recreated by the local Pheasants Forever chapter, and are heavily used by the pheasants.

to high densities then these four different things must be provided in close proximity to each other. The trick of habitat management is to decide which of the four is in short supply and to create it in the right place.

BUILDING A PHEASANT HEAVEN

If what I have said so far is right, what would be the ideal landscape for producing high wild pheasant densities? Describing such a landscape is a very risky exercise: what follows is by no means proven, and I firmly believe in letting the birds tell one what they want by means of their response to management, rather than relying on any theories. Nevertheless, if I were given a blank piece of farmland, how would I lay out the

landscape to maximise breeding pheasant density without compromising the farming too seriously?

The first thing would be to arrange a few blocks of winter cover. This is not to say that winter cover is the most important component of pheasant habitat, just that starting in the winter provides a useful way of following the birds' annual cycle through in terms of different habitat requirements. During the winter the birds are fairly tolerant of each other, so the best winter habitat can be concentrated in a few strategic areas. In this case I have gone for a few blocks of scrubby woodland, each about 5 acres in size and separated by about 200 yards, a nice distance for the birds to move from their autumn to winter ranges. Although they will move miles if they have to, I feel that movements over longer distances are a sign that some habitat feature is in short supply and expecting the birds to move too far exposes them to the risk of predation. The woods need only be large clumps of shrubs, as the birds are really interested in dense cover between about 1 and 6 feet tall. Planting a big area with shrubs is an expensive business and I am not suggesting planting the whole 5 acres as a uniform block. The shrubs should be concentrated around the edges to keep out the wind while the centre can contain open glades or even wide rides to let in some light. The basic idea is to keep the wind out and let the sun in. Tall trees are not important for pheasants and can attract predators, but depending on the part of the world, a few clumps of tall dense conifers may be good for roosting. This would be the case in Britain, but in North America and much of Europe I would avoid them. Of course, if the area is to be used for driven shooting then the precise siting of the winter cover is of crucial importance to the way in which the birds can be shot. It should include flushing areas so the birds can take flight without having to fight their way through the canopy. I am no expert on the different ways in which birds can be driven, or how the woods should be best laid out to help this. But for the sake of this example let us assume that I have sought advice from a professional and woodland is well laid out for driving; it makes little difference to the rest of the scheme. The last item needed would be feed hoppers in the warmest parts of the woods. This is not just to keep the birds well fed but to stop them wandering off and running the risk of predation while searching for their own food.

Once the winter cover has been planted, the next feature would be sites for territories. While the birds will set up territories around the edges of the winter cover, they are much less tolerant of each other in spring so one cannot just rely on these. Some birds will set up territories in clumps of tall grass etc., but to build up really high breeding densities and stop too many birds dispersing elsewhere to breed, I think it is best to lay out strips and clumps of shrubs to act as territories. The size of the shrub areas necessary to provide territories seems to vary around the world. In Britain they must be quite large, while in some of the more open parts of North America they probably do not need to be so big. I have gone for 10 yard wide strips of shrubs with clumps of about 1/10 acre as a reasonable compromise. These would be planted in much the same way as the winter cover; indeed they may also hold birds during milder winters. The trick when providing territories is to maximise the length of edge that they provide and to spread them over the area. These strips should also have a high component of shrubs to maximise their

attractiveness as territories, in just the same way as winter cover.

Once the hens have dispersed from the winter cover to their chosen male's territory, their next concern is to find somewhere to nest. While the shrub areas can be attractive, I would also like to see other, more open nesting cover nearby. As I have said, the hens do not move very far from the territory to nest so I have included areas of uncut grass to help with nesting. As thin strips are particularly vulnerable to predators I have gone for either a width of about 5 yards, or clumps of grasses to avoid the problem. The important thing is that the positioning of the nesting cover is based on where the territories are likely to be; there is no point planting great swathes of nesting cover or sticking it well away from the territories, as the hens will never use it.

An example of how to create good pheasant habitat. Starting with a bare piece of farmland (1), plant a series of small shrubby woodlands (2) and then link these together with belts of shrub (3). Along these edges plant strips and blocks of nesting cover (4) and surround these with good foraging areas for the chicks (5).

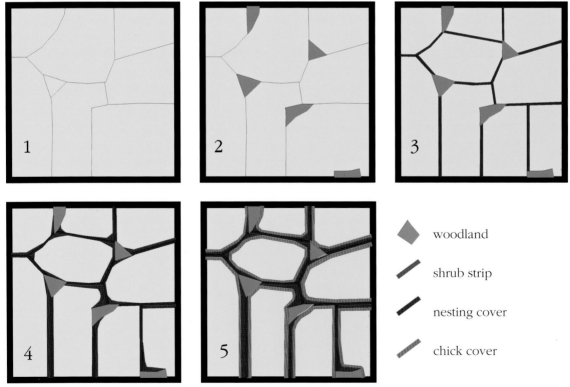

◆ woodland

╱ shrub strip

╱ nesting cover

╱ chick cover

The fourth and final habitat that the birds need is brood-rearing cover. Up to now we have been dealing with adult birds which can move 100 yards or so to find what they are looking for. With the chicks we want the brood-rearing areas to be right next to the nesting cover so that when they hatch they can walk straight out into a suitable habitat. The best chick-feeding cover types in heavily farmed landscapes are the crops themselves, particularly cereals such as wheat and barley, but only if they are managed to leave a smattering of weeds around the edges – Conservation Headlands. In parts of North America or other areas with dry summers, sparse grassy areas, mixtures of bunch grasses and alfalfa work well and may also be good for the chicks, but this does not work in wetter climates. Conservation Headlands are certainly good, but there is also scope to use set-aside to create weedy areas for the chicks; a mix of cereals and other broadleaved crops can work wonders instead.

Once the four habitat types are in place, the next thing to consider is how the birds will actually be managed. The first thing would be to employ a gamekeeper, or at least to find hunters who would be willing to control the most important predators during the nesting season. As with everything else the importance of particular predators will vary according to the part of the world concerned, but the first will be foxes and, to protect the eggs, crows and magpies. Other species such as skunks and racoons may also come into the equation but if foxes and crows are under control then pheasants should thrive. As I mentioned earlier, I only believe in predator control if it does not endanger the predator itself. We are not talking about killing everything that might eat a pheasant or its chicks, just those common species that can legally be controlled and the ones which do the most damage, at the time of year when they actually do the damage. There are also many ways of reducing the impact of predators without actually killing them, for instance by avoiding tall trees in areas with large birds of prey, or by planting wide nesting strips to reduce the searching efficiency of mammals. If pheasant management is being carried out on small discrete areas, there is also scope to reduce the predator density by getting rid of open drains that may provide denning sites and rubbish tips

that may increase their food supply. Whatever approach is taken the idea is to reduce the importance of predation through habitat management and then, within the law, to limit the effects of the common predators during the nesting period.

Depending on the area I would also consider putting out feed hoppers in each cock's territory in the spring to supplement the hens' diet. This may not always be necessary to get them in good condition for breeding, but it does seem to increase breeding densities. A look at a few birds or their droppings would also indicate whether they had a problem with parasitic worms, in which case a suitable drug mixed with the feed might be a good idea in the spring. These last two ideas have yet to be tested in the field but individually they seem to benefit reared birds and may be worth considering for wild stocks as well if they are found to suffer excessive weight loss during the spring.

So far I have only considered the pheasants and not the farming. There is little point having a lot of pheasants if the farmer then goes bankrupt. In the examples I have drawn, the area of land devoted to pheasants amounts to less than 10 per cent of the total area. If this were all taken from productive land then it would obviously be unsustainable, but every farm has awkward corners that can be taken out of production. Remember that we started off here with an area farmed to the corners. Also, both European and North American farmers are now used to the idea of land set-aside from agriculture to reduce surpluses and to protect the environment in other ways. These can all be utilised in ways that will benefit pheasants; the best example is the use of set-aside on Seefeld to plant cereal mixes. Lastly, pheasants are not a species that many conservationists are likely to get exited about, or that governments are going to spend money on conserving. If hunters want to see high densities of wild birds around then they must accept the responsibility of paying for their production. Government grants may soften the blow, and many farmland conservation measures for other purposes can also benefit this bird, but hunters must be willing and able to work with the farmers if pheasants are to thrive.

I will end this book with a final question. Why, as a non-hunter, do I promote pheasant management? The answer lies in the example above.

Hunters are willing to devote time and money to improving farmland habitats, be it through licence fees or voluntary contributions to management or conservation organisations in America, or the creation of woodlands and game-crops for wild or released birds in Britain. An interest in promoting pheasants helps create and pay for a more diverse farmland environment.

I once spent a day touring an estate where the owner was keen to improve his wild pheasant stocks. We took a walk through his woods and I suggested various forms of felling, replanting and ride creation to diversify what were bare, even-aged commercial woodlands. As we went he asked me why, as a non-hunter, I was interested in pheasants. I in turn asked him if he would have considered my advice if I were a butterfly specialist. 'Of course not,' he answered. 'I wouldn't consider spending all this money on butterflies.'

'But the management I am suggesting for pheasants in these woods is exactly what I would also recommend for butterflies,' I answered. 'The only difference is that you will pay for one and not the other, both still benefit.'

I believe that encouraging habitat management for pheasants is a powerful way of increasing the conservation value of farmland. In an ideal world farmers and governments would be willing to create wildlife habitats on farmland for their own sake. Of course some do, but all too often the demands of economics, agricultural intensification and the subsidy systems lead to losses in diversity and an impoverishment of one of our most widespread habitat types – farmland. Habitat management for game can go some way to redressing this.

As a final note I would like to quote from a recent survey of farmers and landowners in Britain. Christopher Short and his colleagues compared the percentage of farmers conducting different forms of habitat management for game and wildlife on their land, splitting the sample into those that released pheasants and those that did not. On those areas where pheasants were released the owners were three times as likely to have planted new woodlands in the last five years, four times as likely to have planted areas of shrub, seven times as likely to have created large rides in their woodlands and nine times as likely to have carried out coppicing. These

figures amount to a considerable private investment in habitat creation. They are all techniques likely to improve the wildlife value of farmland and are an integral part of pheasant management.

An interest in pheasants can be a great incentive for hunters, farmers and landowners to create and maintain wildlife habitats.

Pheasants, despite being voted the most hated bird in Britain, may play an important role in conserving the habitats of many other species. This is one of their main attractions to me.

Index